Lynette's Best-Loved Stitcheries

13 COTTAGE-STYLE PROJECTS YOU'LL ADORE

LYNETTE ANDERSON

Martingale
Create with Confidence

Lynette's Best-Loved Stitcheries:
13 Cottage-Style Projects You'll Adore
© 2019 by Lynette Anderson

Martingale®
19021 120th Ave. NE, Ste. 102
Bothell, WA 98011-9511 USA
ShopMartingale.com

Printed in China
24 23 22 21 20 19   8 7 6 5 4 3 2 1

Library of Congress Cataloging-in-Publication Data
is available upon request.

ISBN: 978-1-68356-012-8

MISSION STATEMENT

We empower makers who use fabric and yarn to make life more enjoyable.

CREDITS

PUBLISHER AND
CHIEF VISIONARY OFFICER
Jennifer Erbe Keltner

CONTENT DIRECTOR
Karen Costello Soltys

DESIGN MANAGER
Adrienne Smitke

MANAGING EDITOR
Tina Cook

PRODUCTION MANAGER
Regina Girard

ACQUISITIONS AND
DEVELOPMENT EDITOR
Laurie Baker

COVER DESIGNER
Kathy Kotomaimoce

COPY EDITOR
Durby Peterson

BOOK DESIGNER
Angie Hoogensen

PHOTOGRAPHER
Brent Kane

ILLUSTRATOR
Sandy Loi

DEDICATION

Thank you to my parents, Ruth and David Law, for the amazing childhood that has been the inspiration behind so many of my designs. xox

Contents

THERE'S MORE ONLINE!

*Visit ShopMartingale.com/LynettesBestLovedStitcheries
for a free, downloadable pillow pattern!*

Introduction

I have had so much fun gathering and selecting the projects for this book. My favorite things to design and stitch are small, useful day-to-day items. It seems, too, that I often need a homemade gift or something special to swap at a sewing retreat, and I always keep that in mind when designing small projects.

I believe the best gifts reflect the maker, so I put a lot of love and care into their creation. For me, ideas for new projects often begin with a memory from childhood. I grew up in a small country village in England, playing in the woods and fields around our home where wildlife and flowers were plentiful. I love to draw the traditional way—with pencil, paper, and eraser—and once I'm happy with a design, I ink the lines and transfer them onto my fabric. I take great joy in selecting the fabrics and embroidery threads. I also love deciding which little details to appliqué, and you'll find my tutorial on Apliquick—my favorite turned-edge method—in this book. And then, of course, comes the stitching. Stitching time is my dreaming time. As I carefully gathered this collection of projects, my hope was that the creative process, from fabric to finish, would be your joy and dreaming time too.

Within these pages you'll find some of my favorite small creations: pillows, little framed delights, a sweet needle case with the tiniest prairie points (page 54), a gorgeous sewing caddy (page 42), and so much more.

Which one will inspire you to begin stitching first?

General Techniques

The projects I've selected represent many of my favorite designs and also my go-to techniques—some tried and true, some developed with tools I've come to love. In this section we'll cover methods and materials along with an embroidery stitch guide for your reference as you stitch the projects. For any project you want to make, please read all the instructions before starting. Remember that careful and accurate cutting and sewing will ensure success.

Apliquick Method for Turned-Edge Appliqué

Through the years I've used several methods to appliqué my projects, and after much trial and error, the technique I prefer now is the Apliquick method using Apliquick rods and semi-water-soluble paper. All of the appliquéd projects in this book can be made using this turned-edge technique for lovely results. Of course, if you prefer, you may use needle-turn appliqué, fusible appliqué, or another favorite appliqué technique. All of the appliqué patterns in this book have been reversed for Apliquick or fusible appliqué methods.

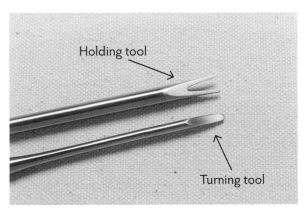

Two Apliquick rods are used—one with a pronged end to hold the appliqué shapes steady and one with a tapered end to roll and press turned edges.

SUPPLIES

For the Apliquick method, you'll need all of the following supplies; my favorite brands are shown in parentheses, but feel free to use what works best for you.

Fabric for appliqués

Apliquick rods

Fabric scissors (Karen Kay Buckley's 4" Perfect Scissors)

Pencil for tracing appliqué patterns (Apliquick pencil or 2B drawing pencil)

Appliqué paper, semi-water-soluble (Hugs 'N Kisses)

Fabric glue pen, water-soluble

Basting glue, water-soluble (Roxanne Glue-Baste-It) or appliqué pins

Fine gold-eye needles (Lynette Anderson Designs) or No. 9 gold-eye appliqué needles (Clover)

Fine-weight thread to match appliqué fabrics (100-weight by Lynette Anderson Designs or 60-weight Bottom Line by Superior Threads)

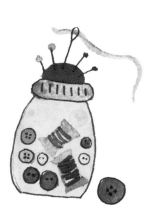

Having these tools at the ready will give you a great start for stitching success.

HOW TO APLIQUICK

1 Trace each reversed appliqué pattern onto the nonshiny side of the appliqué paper.

2 Cut out each shape on the drawn line.

3 Place each shape, fusible side down, on the wrong side of the appropriate fabric. If you have more than one shape cut from the same fabric, leave at least ¼" between shapes. Fuse in place with a hot, dry iron. Cut out each shape a scant ¼" beyond the perimeter of the appliqué paper.

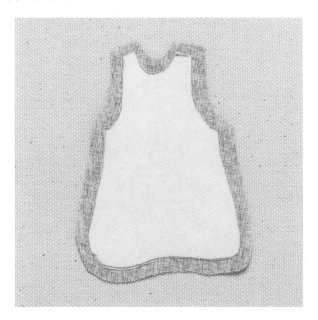

4 If the appliqué shape has embroidery details, turn it to the right side and use a brown fine-tip Pigma pen to trace the embroidery design onto the front of the appliqué. With the aid of a light source, you should see the outline of the design shadowing through from the back.

5 Clip all concave (inward) curves of the fabric shape just to the paper edge; clipping will help ensure that the curves are smooth once you turn under the edges.

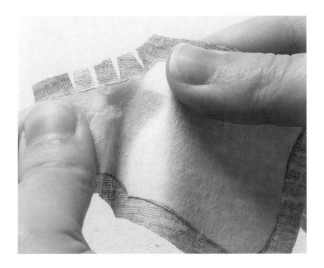

6 Using the forked Apliquick rod in your nondominant hand to hold the shape in place, use the glue pen to apply glue to a small section on the edge of the appliqué paper and just slightly onto the fabric seam allowance.

7 Holding the tapered Apliquick rod in your dominant hand and the forked rod in your other hand, roll and press the seam allowance from the front to the back, where the glue will hold it in place. If the glue dries while you're working, apply more as needed.

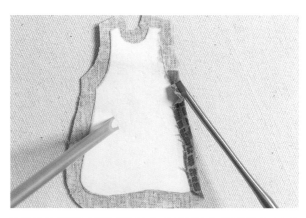

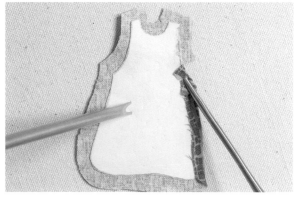

GENERAL TECHNIQUES

8 Once you've turned and secured the entire seam allowance of each appliqué, press the appliqué from the wrong side, then the right side. Then position the appliqués on the background. Baste them in place using water-soluble glue, pins, or thread. I prefer to glue baste, so I can avoid thread catching on pins (see page 17).

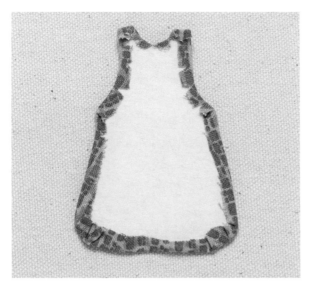

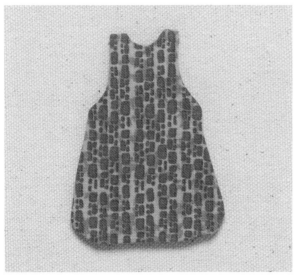

9 Hand stitch the appliqués using an appliqué stitch.

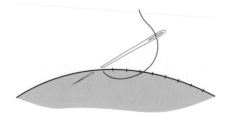

Appliqué stitch

Fusible Appliqué

For tiny pieces, it's often easiest to use fusible appliqué.

1 Trace the reversed appliqué pattern onto the paper side of the fusible web, leaving enough space around the shape to roughly cut out ½" around the perimeter.

2 Follow the manufacturer's instructions to fuse the fusible-web piece to the wrong side of the appliqué fabric. Let cool; peel away the paper backing.

3 Place the appliqué on the project, right side up. If the appliqué piece abuts another appliqué piece, be sure to note which pieces will overlap. Dashed lines on the designs indicate this. Fuse the appliqué in place with a medium-hot iron.

4 Hand or machine stitch around the appliqué edge using a blanket stitch, satin stitch, or tiny whipstitch.

English-Paper-Pieced Hexagons

Each project featuring hexagons includes a pattern for cutting fabric hexagons and a pattern for cutting paper hexagons. To save time, use purchased hexagon shapes made from precut cardstock or semi-water-soluble fusible-appliqué paper. Whether you use purchased shapes or you cut them yourself, the process for using them and the results are the same.

1 To cut the fabric hexagons, use the pattern provided to make a template from template plastic or cardstock. Use the template to trace the number of hexagons listed for each project onto the wrong side of the fabrics. The seam allowance is included in the pattern. Cut out each fabric shape on the marked lines.

2 If you're not using precut paper hexagons, use the paper hexagon pattern provided to trace and cut out the number of paper hexagons required from lightweight cardstock or semi-water-soluble fusible paper (this is the same paper I use to make my Apliquick shapes). If cutting them yourself, cut exactly on the traced line; the more accurately you cut, the more easily the pieces will fit together.

3 Center a paper hexagon on the wrong side of a fabric hexagon. Pin in place or use a glue pen to lightly attach the center of the paper shape to the fabric shape.

4 One side at a time, fold the seam allowance to the back of the paper liner and thread baste or lightly

glue baste the fabric edges over the paper hexagons. Fold the edges tautly so there is no extra give, but without distorting the fabric. Gently press. Repeat to prepare the number of hexagons required for the project.

5   Place two basted fabric hexagons right sides together with one flat edge aligned. Whipstitch the edges together, taking tiny stitches through the fabric, *not* through the paper. Keep the stitches close together, gently pulling the threads into place. Continue joining hexagons as indicated in the project instructions.

6   When the hexagons are all joined, carefully remove the cardstock papers by clipping the basting threads or simply peeling the papers away if they've been glue basted. You do not need to remove hexagons made from appliqué paper. The light glue baste makes this step simple. Press gently.

Embroidery

For each project I've included an embroidery guide with the stitches I used. Although I rely on my go-to stitches, embroidery can be fun and eclectic. Use the stitches that suit your fancy. I am not a hoop user, because I like the feel and control of having the fabric in my hands, but I do use a thimble when I embroider.

TRANSFERRING EMBROIDERY DESIGNS

For light- to medium-colored background fabrics, tape the embroidery pattern onto a light source, such as a light box or window, then place the fabric right side up over the pattern. Using a fine-tip fabric marker, trace the embroidery pattern onto the background fabric.

For dark background fabrics, trace the embroidery design onto the nonsticky side of a stick-on dissolvable stabilizer, such as Solvy Sticky Fabri-Solvy. Remove the release sheet and stick the traced stabilizer directly onto the right side of the fabric to be embroidered. Embroider through the stabilizer and fabric. Once complete, follow the manufacturer's instructions for dissolving stabilizer.

For tracing, I use only a fine-tip brown Pigma pen. The ink is permanent, but it leaves a very fine line that is easy to cover with embroidery floss. If you're not comfortable using permanent ink, try the Solvy method or use a removable marking pen with a fine point.

PREVENTING THREAD SHADOWING

You can prevent embroidery threads on the back of the work from shadowing through to the front by fusing embroidery stabilizer to the wrong side of light fabrics. I always use fusible stabilizer (my own brand, of course!) behind my embroidery and appliqué. When using fusible embroidery stabilizer, you'll need to press it onto the wrong side of the background fabric, following the manufacturer's instructions before you begin stitching. Turn the piece over and press from the right side as well, to ensure a good bond. Let the fabric cool before handling. I also apply a lightweight fusible stabilizer to the wrong side of any cotton fabrics that will be backed with a fusible batting, especially for bags; the stabilizer leaves a smoother finish on the right side of the project.

fabric and thread

EMBROIDERY STITCH GUIDE

If you encounter any unfamiliar stitches in this book,
follow the illustrations below.

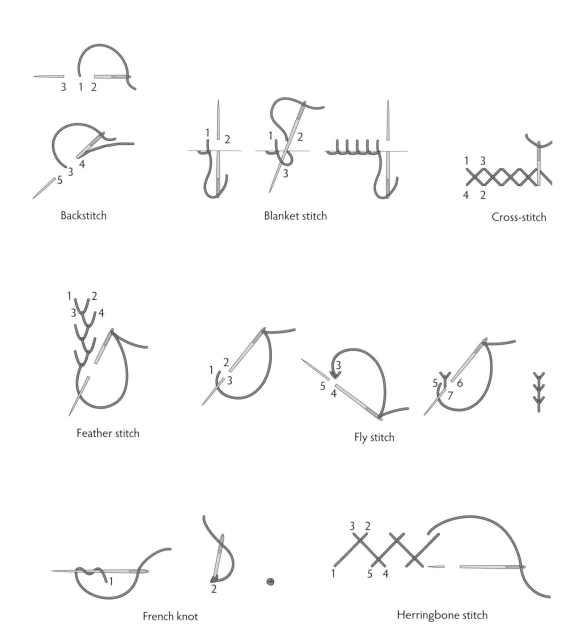

Backstitch

Blanket stitch

Cross-stitch

Feather stitch

Fly stitch

French knot

Herringbone stitch

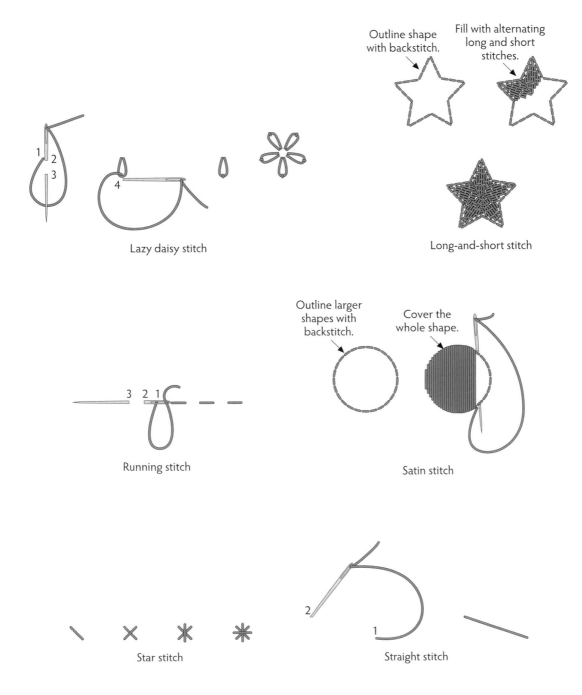

Outline shape with backstitch.

Fill with alternating long and short stitches.

Long-and-short stitch

Lazy daisy stitch

Outline larger shapes with backstitch.

Cover the whole shape.

Running stitch

Satin stitch

Star stitch

Straight stitch

Sunshine and Flowers Pillow

Decorate a pillow with a darling appliquéd angel who is busy watering her embroidered garden. More for admiring than for napping, the pillow offers a delightful assortment of stitchery motifs and a hand-painted watering-can button.

FINISHED SIZE
15½" × 15½"

Materials

In addition to the following materials, you'll need supplies for your favorite appliqué method. Supplies for the Apliquick method used for this project are given on page 7.

10" × 10" square of cream tone on tone for embroidery background

5" × 6" rectangle of mauve print for dress

3" × 4" scrap of medium blue print for apron

7" × 15" rectangle of teal print for inner border and apron pocket

14" × 18" rectangle of light blue print for outer border

16" × 16" square of coordinating print for pillow back

1¼" × 1½" watering-can button (YB346 Green Watering Can from Lynette Anderson Designs)

2 beige 5 mm 2-hole buttons

Polyester fiberfill for stuffing

10" × 10" square of fusible embroidery stabilizer, optional

Brown fine-tip fabric marker

Water-soluble basting glue, optional

Embroidery Floss

The colors listed below are for Cosmo 6-strand embroidery floss.

Brown (#2311) for angel's shoes, birdhouse post, and wood grain

Charcoal (#895) for outer frame, bee, birds' eyes, seed packet, garden fork, angel's face, and beehive door and detail

Eggplant (#765) for angel's wings and large and small daisies

Gold (#575) for words, bee, beehive outline, birds' beaks, halo, and small-daisy centers

Green (#634) for flower stems and leaves, halo leaves, birdhouse roofs and bands, and inner-box frame

Light blue (#2981) for birds, shoelaces, halo flowers, and small daisy

Medium eggplant (#763) for small daisy and halo flowers

Putty (#713) for head, hand and leg outlines, and bee's wings

Rose (#655) for halo flowers, large-daisy center, birdcage heart, pot, inner-box frame outline, outer-frame Xs, and outer-border edging

Cutting

From the teal print, cut:
2 strips, 1½" × 11"
2 strips, 1½" × 9"
1 square, 2" × 2"

From the light blue print, cut:
2 strips, 3" × 16"
2 strips, 3" × 11"

Preparing the Background

1. Referring to "Apliquick Method for Turned-Edge Appliqué" on page 7, prepare the dress, apron, and apron pocket for turned-edge appliqué using appliqué paper and the patterns on page 18. Do *not* cut out the appliqué shapes. Trace the embroidery details onto the right side of the traced apron fabric. Refer to "Transferring Embroidery Designs" on page 11 for additional information.

2. Referring to the embroidery key on page 19, embroider the seed packet and fork on the traced apron, noting the stitches used.

3. Cut out the pocket ¼" outside the marked perimeter and complete the appliqué shape using the Apliquick method.

4. Position the pocket appliqué so the finished top edge will cover the bottom of the embroidery stitches on the apron fabric. Baste the pocket in place using pins, thread, or basting glue. Appliqué the pocket in place. Cut out the apron and the dress ¼" outside the marked perimeter and complete the appliqué using the Apliquick method.

5. Using the placement and embroidery patterns on pages 19 and 20 and the brown marker, trace the embroidery design so that it's centered on the cream 10" square.

6 Position the dress appliqué on the cream square, referring to the pattern on page 19 for placement. Baste and appliqué in place as for the apron pocket. Repeat to add the apron.

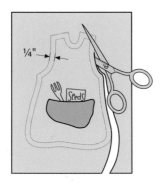

1/4"

7 If using optional fusible embroidery stabilizer, fuse it to the wrong side of the cream square.

Embroidering the Square

Referring to the embroidery key on page 19, embroider the entire traced design on the cream square, using two strands of floss and noting the stitches used. Once the

embroidery is complete, press the work and trim the square to 9" × 9", centering the design.

Making the Pillow

Use ¼" seam allowances. Press seam allowances as indicated by the arrows.

1 Join teal 1½" × 9" strips to opposite sides of the embroidered square. Join the two remaining teal strips to the top and bottom. The unit should measure 11" square, including seam allowances.

Make 1 unit,
11" × 11".

2 Join light blue 3" × 11" strips to opposite sides of the unit from step 1. Join the two remaining light blue strips to the top and bottom to complete the pillow front, which should measure 16" square, including seam allowances.

Make 1 unit,
16" × 16".

SUNSHINE AND FLOWERS PILLOW

3 Place the pillow back square and pillow front right sides together and stitch around the edge, leaving a 4" opening to turn the pillow right side out. Clip the corners.

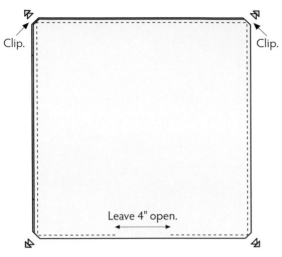

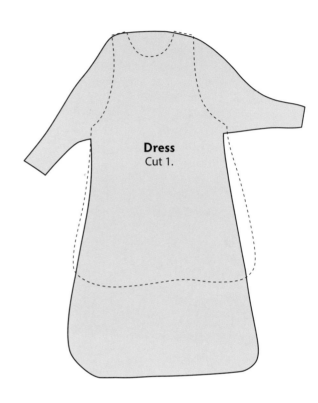

4 Turn the pillow right side out. Carefully push out the corners. Gently press.

5 With two strands of rose floss and starting at one side of the opening, work a running stitch ¼" inside the pillow edge. Stitch around the pillow. When you reach the other side of the opening, leave enough of a thread tail to finish stitching once the pillow is stuffed.

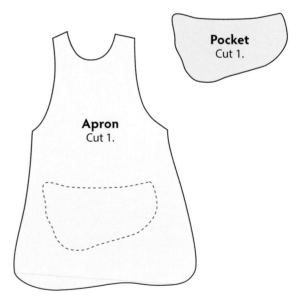

6 Sew the watering-can button to the angel's hand and sew the beige buttons to her apron.

7 Stuff the completed pillow with fiberfill. Stitch the opening closed and complete the running stitch.

Embroidery Key

— Backstitch

✕ Cross-stitch

• French knot

◯ Lazy daisy

- - - Running stitch

■ Satin stitch

Sunshine and flowers

Button placement

Satin stitch

Fill with French knots.

Satin stitch

Seeds

Join to Placement and Embroidery Pattern: Right (page 20) along this line to complete pattern.

Placement and Embroidery Pattern: Left

SUNSHINE AND FLOWERS PILLOW

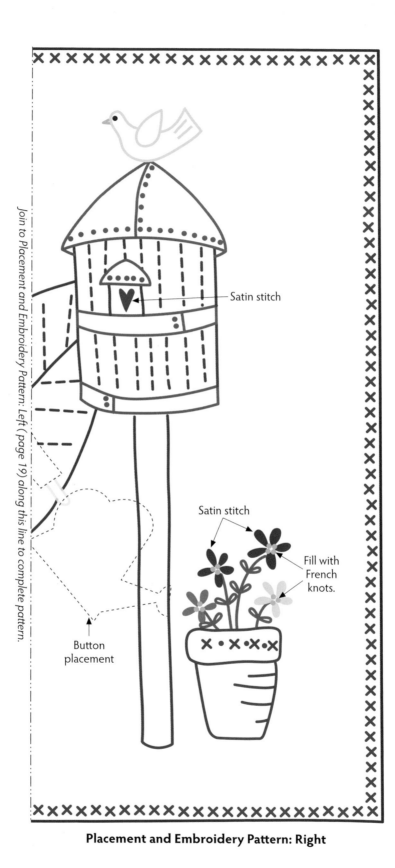

Join to Placement and Embroidery Pattern: Left (page 19) along this line to complete pattern.

Satin stitch

Satin stitch

Fill with French knots.

Button placement

Placement and Embroidery Pattern: Right

Meadow Cottage Tote

Capture an idyllic spring day complete with a charming thatched
cottage and a stream meandering through the meadow. Enjoy making
a colorful quilted tote that's sure to be a conversation starter.

FINISHED SIZE
14" × 14"

Materials

*Yardage is based on 42"-wide fabric. In addition to the
following materials, you'll need supplies for your favorite
appliqué method. Supplies for the Apliquick method used
for this project are given on page 7.*

8" × 8" square of cream tone on tone for embroidery
background

5" × 5" square of red print for roof

5" × 5" square of lavender print for cottage

Small scrap of olive print for door

5" × 5" square of light blue print for clouds

16 strips, 1½" × 14½" *each,* of assorted coordinating
prints for bag front

7 strips, 2½" × 14½" *each,* of assorted coordinating
prints for bag back

½ yard of blue print for bag base and handles

¾ yard of coordinating print for lining and inside pocket

18" × 36" piece of thin batting

14½" × 32½" rectangle of lightweight fusible interfacing

⅝" × ⅞" bluebird button (YB366 Heart and Bird Button
Pack from Lynette Anderson Designs)

⅜" speckled heart button (YB366 Heart and Bird Button
Pack from Lynette Anderson Designs)

8" × 8" square of fusible embroidery stabilizer, optional

Brown fine-tip fabric marker

Spray adhesive, optional

Temporary basting glue, optional

Embroidery Floss

*The colors listed below are for Valdani 6-strand,
hand-dyed embroidery floss.*

Black (#0511) for roof detail

Brown variegated (#518) for tree, hill, stones, and bird's
legs and eye

Dark red (#078) for chimneys, heart on front door,
and daisy centers

Gold (#154) for bird's beak and sun

Lavender (#8103) for windows and corner of house

Continued on page 23

Continued from page 21

Light blue variegated (#JP12) for stream, cloud detail, heart button string, and bird

Light green (#0576) for hill underline, stems, leaves, and Xs in meadow

Purple (#P10) for daisies and tree blossoms

Cutting

From the blue print, cut:
2 strips, 4½" × 42"
1 rectangle, 4½" × 14½"

From the coordinating print for lining and inside pocket, cut:
1 rectangle, 14½" × 32"
2 rectangles, 6½" × 10"

Preparing the Background

1. Referring to "Apliquick Method for Turned-Edge Appliqué" on page 7, prepare the roof, cottage, door, and cloud for turned-edge appliqué using the patterns on page 28. Do *not* cut out the appliqué shapes.

2. Trace the embroidery details (page 29) onto the right side of the prepared shapes using the brown marker and light source. Refer to "Transferring Embroidery Designs" on page 11 for additional information.

3. Cut out the roof, cottage, door, and clouds ¼" outside the marked perimeter and complete the appliqué shapes using the Apliquick method.

4. Using the placement and embroidery pattern on page 29, trace the embroidery design onto the cream square, centering the design.

5. Position the cottage on the cream square, referring to the placement and embroidery pattern. Baste it in place using pins, thread, or basting glue.

6. Appliqué the cottage in place, followed by the roof, door, and clouds.

7. If using optional fusible embroidery stabilizer, fuse it to the wrong side of the cream square after the appliqué is complete.

Embroidering the Square

Referring to the embroidery key on page 29, embroider the tree, bird, sun, ground and ground details, brook, and appliqué details using two strands of floss. Once the embroidery is complete, press the work and trim the cream square to 6½" × 6½", centering the design.

VARIEGATED STRAND LENGTHS

The subtle variations within each skein of Valdani hand-dyed floss are beautiful. When working on small areas of embroidery, I recommend cutting two short lengths of floss (approximately 10") to get nice color variation. Label the lengths A and B. Start the embroidery by working with two strands of A. Take a few stitches or complete a design element, such as a flower petal, and then switch to strand B. Keep alternating to get the effect you desire.

Making the Tote Front and Back

Use ¼" seam allowances unless otherwise indicated. Press seam allowances toward the piece just added.

1. Join the 1½" × 14½" strips to the embroidered square, beginning on the bottom of the square and working clockwise. After joining each piece, trim the ends of the piece even with the center square. Once you've sewn a strip to each side, check that the unit measures 8½" square, including seam allowances.

Make 1 unit, 8½" × 8½".

2 Add three more rounds of strips to the embroidered square, starting at the bottom and ending at the right side of the square each round. After the second round, the unit should measure 10½" square. After the third round, the unit should measure 12½" square. After the last strip, the finished front should measure 14½" square, including seam allowances.

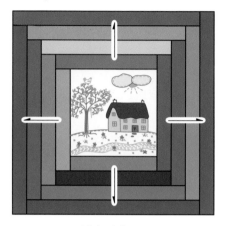

Make 1 front,
14½" × 14½".

3 To make the bag back, arrange and join the seven assorted 2½" × 14½" strips. The bag back should measure 14½" square, including seam allowances.

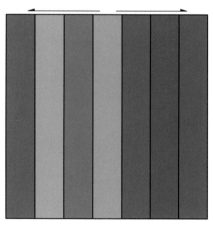

Make 1 back,
14½" × 14½".

Assembling the Tote

1 Join the bag front to the top of the blue 4½" × 14½" bag base. With the strips oriented vertically, join the bag back to the bottom of the bag base. The unit should measure 14½" × 32½", including seam allowances.

2 Fuse the lightweight interfacing to the wrong side of the unit; this helps give a softer appearance to the finished bag than just a layer of batting.

3 Layer the bag and batting. If desired, spray the batting with temporary spray adhesive to hold the layers together while quilting.

4 Quilt by hand or machine. The bag shown is machine quilted with a single line of stitching in the center of each log-cabin strip on the front and with two rows of straight stitching along each strip on the back. Trim the quilted unit to 14½" × 32". Carefully trim ¼" of batting from the top and bottom edges without clipping the threads or fabric.

5 To make the handles, fold the two blue 4½"-wide strips in half lengthwise and finger-press to crease. Open out and fold the long raw edges inward to meet at the crease line; press. Fold in half again; press. Topstitch close to both edges and add a third row of topstitching through the center of each strip. Trim each strip to 32" long.

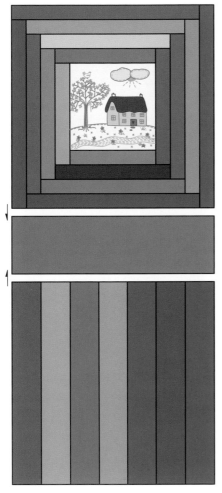

Make 1 unit,
14½" × 32½".

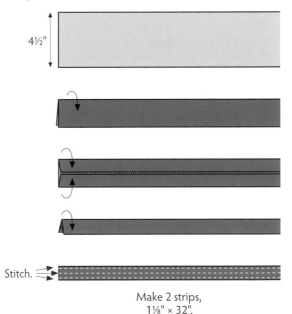

4½"

Stitch.

Make 2 strips,
1⅛" × 32".

6 Pin the bag handles in place on the top-right side of the quilted unit, approximately 2½" in from each side, making sure they aren't twisted. Baste the handles in place. Repeat on the bottom of the quilted unit with the handles facing upward.

7 Fold the unit in half, right sides together, sandwiching the handles inside. Stitch from the top to the bottom on each side, backstitching at the beginning and end.

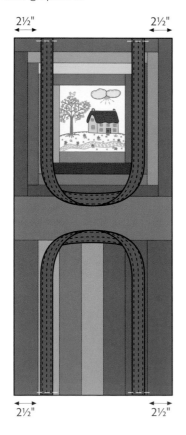

2½"   2½"

2½"   2½"

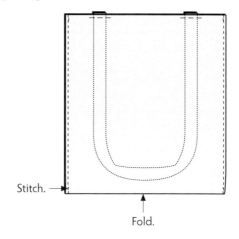

Stitch. →

Fold.

8 To box the bag corners, with the wrong side still out, pull out the bottom corner to form a point, with the side seam allowances folded toward the bag back. Draw a line 2" from the corner point. Sew on the drawn line. Trim off the excess fabric. Repeat for the remaining corner to complete the outer bag.

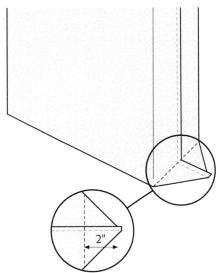

Finishing the Tote

1 To make a pocket, layer and sew the two 6½" × 10" rectangles right sides together, leaving a 2" opening to turn right side out. Clip across the corners and turn right side out through the opening. Carefully push out the corners and hand stitch the opening closed. The pocket should be 6" × 9½". Fold in half so the 6" sides meet; press a crease line.

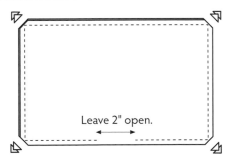

Leave 2" open.

2 Fold the 14½" × 32" lining rectangle in half lengthwise so the 32" sides meet; press a crease line. Align the crease on the pocket with the crease on the lining rectangle, with the pocket approximately 3" from the top edge. Sew close to the edge of the pocket on the side and bottom edges, leaving the top open and backstitching at the beginning and end. Stitch another row approximately ⅛" from the first row to ensure that the pocket is secure. Sew a third line of stitching along the pocket crease if you want to divide the pocket into two smaller sections.

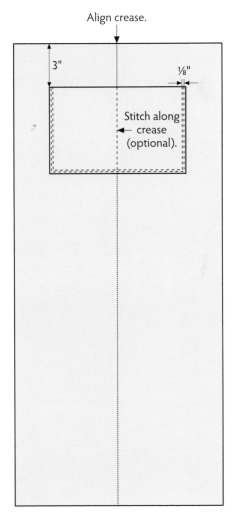

Align crease.

3"

⅛"

Stitch along crease (optional).

3 Fold the lining rectangle with the pocket attached right sides together and stitch the sides, leaving a 4" opening in one side. Box the corners as you did for the outer bag.

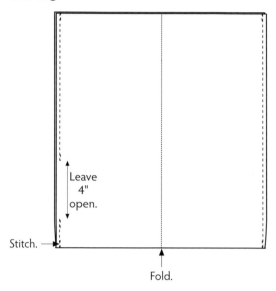

Leave 4" open.

Stitch. →

Fold.

4 With right sides together, insert the lining into the bag, aligning the side seams. Pin along the top edge. Stitch completely around the top edge with a ½" seam allowance.

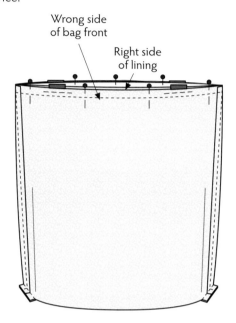

Wrong side of bag front

Right side of lining

5 Turn the bag right side out through the opening in the lining. Press the top of the bag and topstitch around the edge. Hand sew the opening in the bag lining closed. Sew on the bird and heart buttons.

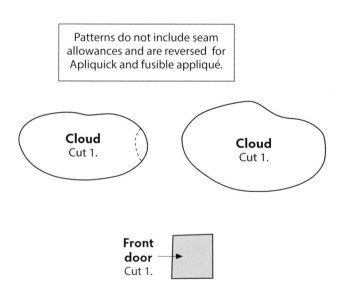

Patterns do not include seam allowances and are reversed for Apliquick and fusible appliqué.

Cloud
Cut 1.

Cloud
Cut 1.

Front door
Cut 1.

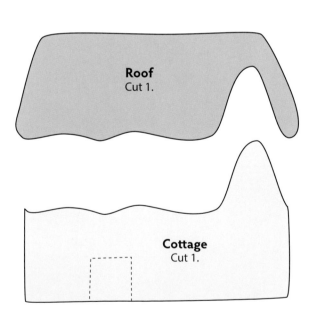

Roof
Cut 1.

Cottage
Cut 1.

LYNETTE'S BEST-LOVED STITCHERIES

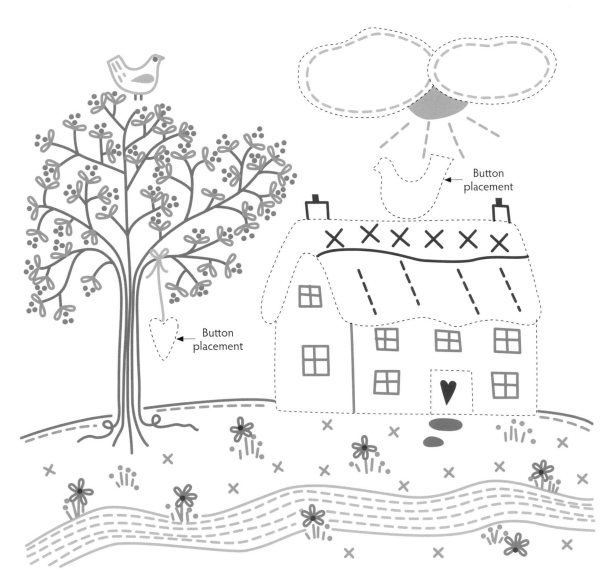

Button
placement

Button
placement

Placement and Embroidery Pattern

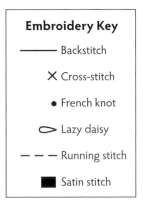

Embroidery Key

—— Backstitch

✕ Cross-stitch

• French knot

◯ Lazy daisy

– – – Running stitch

■ Satin stitch

Redwork Pillow Pair

Redwork is quick, fun, and addictive! Enjoy stitching lovable pillows that team beautifully with the Home Sweet Home Redwork on page 93.

Bee an Angel

FINISHED SIZE
8½" × 10"

Materials

Yardage is based on 42"-wide fabric.

8" × 8" square of cream solid for embroidery background

8 strips, 1½" × 9½" *each*, of assorted red prints for border strips

9" × 10½" rectangle of red print for back

Country red 6-strand embroidery floss (Cosmo #2241)

2 red 5 mm buttons (1 square, 1 circle)

Polyester fiberfill

8" × 8" rectangle of fusible embroidery stabilizer, optional

Brown fine-tip fabric marker

Embroidering the Square

1. Using the Bee an Angel embroidery pattern on page 33, a light source, and the brown marker, center and trace the embroidery design onto the right side of the fabric square. If using optional fusible embroidery stabilizer, fuse it to the wrong side of the fabric once the tracing is complete.

SPECKLE THE BACKGROUND

To dye cream fabric to achieve the speckled effect as shown, follow these simple instructions:

1. *Wet the cream solid square thoroughly, then squeeze out most of the water.*

2. *Lay the square flat and sprinkle generously with tea leaves. You can use a tea bag or loose tea. Long tea leaves create wonderful effects.*

3. *Fold up the fabric square so the leaves are safely inside. Place on a microwave-safe plate and dampen again.*

4. *Microwave on high for two minutes. The fabric will be hot when you take it out, so be cautious. Unfold and check for color density. If you'd like darker markings, dampen again and microwave for two more minutes.*

5. *Once you're pleased with the look of the fabric, shake off the tea leaves; I sprinkle mine in the garden. Rinse well and iron dry. If you want creases for effect, line dry and then press lightly.*

Making the Pillow

Use ¼" seam allowances. Press seam allowances toward the piece just added.

1 Join the 1½" × 9½" red print strips to the embroidered rectangle, beginning on the right side of the rectangle and working counterclockwise. After joining each piece, use a rotary cutter and mat and an acrylic ruler to trim the ends of the piece even with the center rectangle. Once you've joined a strip to each side, check that the unit measures 7" × 8½", including seam allowances.

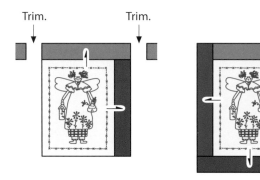

Make 1 unit,
7" × 8½".

2 Add another round of strips to the embroidered rectangle in the same manner. Once all the pieces are joined, press the pillow front. The finished front should measure 9" × 10½", including seam allowances.

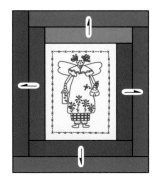

Make 1 unit, 9" × 10½".

2 Referring to the embroidery key on page 33, work all the embroidery in red floss, noting the stitches used. Use one strand of floss for the pantaloon cuffs, beehive lines, birdhouse, hair and face, flower centers, stems, and leaves; use two strands for all other stitches.

3 Once the embroidery is complete, press the square well and trim to 5" × 6½", centering the design.

4 Stitch the round button to the top of the angel's head using red floss. Overlap the square button on the round one and stitch it in place, referring to the pattern for placement.

LYNETTE'S BEST-LOVED STITCHERIES

3 Place the pillow front and back rectangles right sides together and stitch ¼" from the edges, leaving a 4" opening in the bottom for turning. Clip across the corners to reduce bulk.

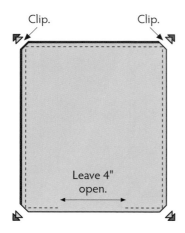

4 Turn the pillow right side out and push out the corners. Gently press, avoiding the buttons.

5 With two strands of red floss, work a running stitch ¼" from the pillow edge. Stitch around the pillow, starting at one side of the opening. When you reach the opposite side of the opening, leave enough of a thread tail to finish stitching once the pillow is stuffed.

6 Stuff the completed pillow with fiberfill. Stitch the opening closed and complete the running stitch.

Bee an Angel Embroidery Pattern

Embroidery Key

——— Backstitch

✕ Cross-stitch

● French knot

⌒ Lazy daisy

– – – Running stitch

Embroidering the Square

1 Refer to "Speckle the Background" on page 30 if you'd like to tea speckle the cream square. Refer to the embroidery instructions on page 30 to complete the embroidered square using the embroidery pattern and key on page 35.

2 Once the embroidery is complete, press the square well and trim to 5" × 6½", centering the design.

Making the Pillow

Use ¼" seam allowances. Press seam allowances toward the piece just added.

1 Refer to steps 1 and 2 of the Bee an Angel pillow on page 32 to add two rounds of red strips to the embroidered rectangle. Follow the placement guide below to add the strips in numerical order, working in a clockwise fashion. The unit should measure 7" × 8½", including seam allowances, after the first round is complete and 9" × 10½" after the second round is complete. Press the pillow front.

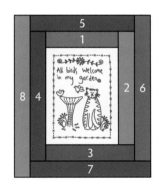

Placement guide

2 Refer to steps 3–6 on page 33 to complete the pillow.

All Birds Welcome

FINISHED SIZE
8½" × 10"

Materials

Yardage is based on 42"-wide fabric.

8" × 8" square of cream solid for embroidery background

8 strips, 1½" × 10½" *each*, of assorted red prints for border strips

9" × 10½" rectangle of red print for back

Country red 6-strand embroidery floss (Cosmo #2241)

Polyester fiberfill

8" × 8" rectangle of fusible embroidery stabilizer, optional

Brown fine-tip fabric marker

All Birds Welcome Embroidery Pattern

Embroidery Key

——— Backstitch

✕ Cross-stitch

● French knot

◯ Lazy daisy

– – – Running stitch

Blossom Tree Wall Hanging

Create a colorful wall hanging where spring is in the air, bees are buzzing, birds are nesting, and blooms are bursting open. Combine simple embroidery stitches with an assortment of fun prints in a border that's easily pieced.

FINISHED SIZE
12½" × 14½"

Materials

Yardage is based on 42"-wide fabric.

12" × 19" rectangle of cream print for background and pieced border

¼ yard *total* of 10 assorted prints for pieced border

⅛ yard of coordinating floral for binding

17" × 19" rectangle of coordinating print for backing

17" × 19" piece of batting

Bee button (YB337 Busy Bees Button Pack from Lynette Anderson Designs)

12" × 19" rectangle of fusible embroidery stabilizer, optional

Brown fine-tip fabric marker

Embroidery Floss

The colors listed below are for Cosmo 6-strand embroidery floss.

Charcoal (#895) for butterfly's body, insects' flight paths and antennae, beehive hole and string, owl's feet, owl and birds' eyes, and dashed ground line

Country blue (#734) for birds, butterfly, dots in sky, and outline

Cream (#364) for dots on owl's chest

Dark chocolate (#3311) for tree

Ginger brown (#2310) for owl and nests

Gold (#575) for beehive, tulip stamens, and owl and birds' beaks

Medium eggplant (#763) for tree blossoms

Olive green (#685) for tree leaves

Raspberry pink (#434) for tulips

Tan (#368) for tulip leaves, words, and details below words

Cutting

From *both* the cream print and the fusible stabilizer (optional), cut:
1 rectangle, 12" × 15"
4 squares, 3" × 3"

From *each* of the 10 assorted prints, cut:
4 rectangles, 1½" × 2" (40 total)

From the coordinating floral, cut:
2 strips, 1½" × 42"

Spring

when the bulbs start to grow
and blossom fills the trees

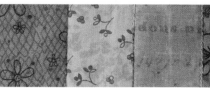
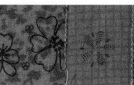

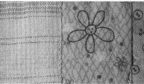

Embroidering the Rectangle

1 Using the placement and embroidery patterns on pages 40 and 41 and the brown marker, trace the embroidery design onto the right side of the cream 12" × 15" rectangle. Using the bird embroidery pattern on page 41, trace the embroidery design onto each cream 3" square, reversing the bird on two of the squares. If using optional fusible embroidery stabilizer, fuse it to the wrong side the fabric pieces once the tracing is complete.

2 Referring to the embroidery key on page 41, work all the embroidery using two strands of floss, noting the stitches used.

3 Once you've completed the embroidery, press well. Trim the embroidered tree rectangle to 9½" × 11½", centering the design. Trim each of the embroidered bird squares to 2" × 2", centering the birds in their squares.

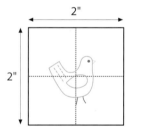
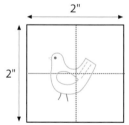

Make 2 of each unit.

Making the Patchwork Border

Use ¼" seam allowances. Press seam allowances as indicated by the arrows.

1 On a work surface, lay out the embroidered rectangle with an embroidered bird square positioned at each corner as shown. Place nine print rectangles at the top and bottom of the rectangle and 11 print rectangles on each side between the bird squares.

Arrange the prints as desired, making sure the 2" sides of the rectangles are adjacent to each other and the birds face toward the center.

2 Working on one side at a time, join the print rectangles on each side of the rectangle to make the border strips. Join the bird squares to opposite ends of the top and bottom borders. The side borders should measure 2" × 11½", including seam allowances. The top and bottom borders should measure 2" × 12½", including seam allowances.

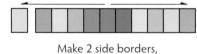

Make 2 side borders,
2" × 11½".

Make 2 top/bottom borders,
2" × 12½".

3 Join the side borders to the sides of the embroidered tree rectangle. Join the top and bottom borders to the top and bottom edges to complete the wall-hanging top, which should measure 12½" × 14½", including seam allowances.

Wall-hanging assembly

Finishing the Wall Hanging

For more detailed information about any finishing steps, visit ShopMartingale.com/HowtoQuilt.

1 Layer the wall-hanging top, batting, and backing; baste the layers together. Quilt by hand or machine. The wall hanging shown is machine quilted with simple in-the-ditch stitching.

2 Join the floral 1½"-wide strips end to end to make one long strip and use it to finish the quilt edges with a single-fold binding.

3 Stitch the bee button above the flight path on the right-hand side of the embroidered rectangle where shown on the pattern.

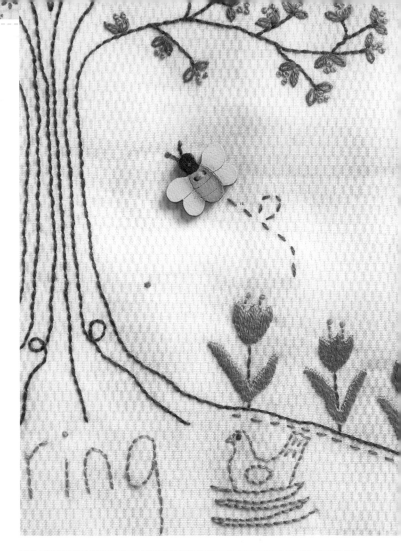

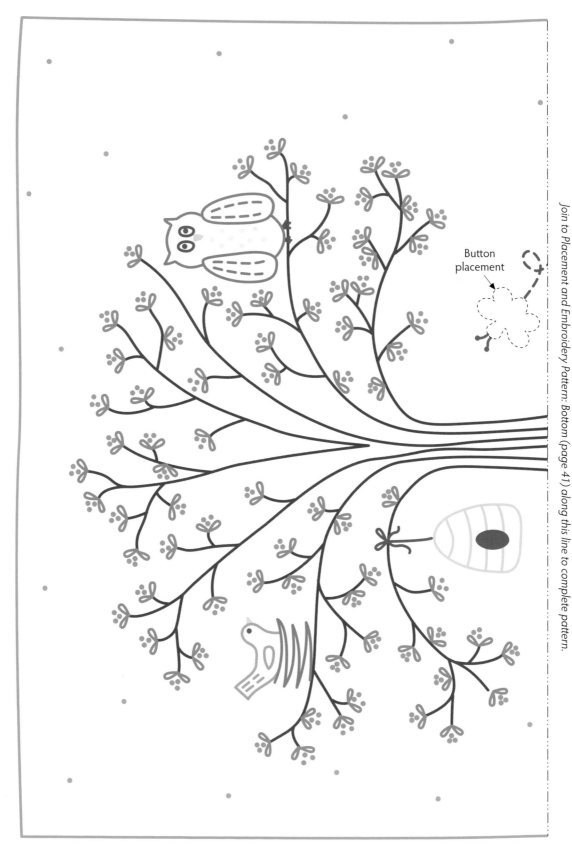

Button
placement

Join to Placement and Embroidery Pattern: Bottom (page 41) along this line to complete pattern.

Blossom Tree Wall Hanging Placement and Embroidery Pattern: Top

Join to Placement and Embroidery Pattern: Top (page 40) along this line to complete pattern.

Spring

When the bulbs start to grow
and blossom fills the trees

Blossom Tree Wall Hanging Placement and Embroidery Pattern: Bottom

Bird
Trace 2 and 2 reversed.

Embroidery Key

——	Backstitch
✕	Cross-stitch
●	French knot
⌒	Lazy daisy
- - -	Running stitch
▬	Satin stitch

One-Stitch-at-a-Time Sewing Caddy

Now here's a sewing caddy and conversation piece that you'll adore and all your sewing friends will covet. Ready to accommodate all your sewing passions, the caddy features a cute appliquéd sewing machine and Gran's button jar, plus English-paper-pieced hexagons on the back.

FINISHED SIZE
8" wide × 6" tall × 3¾" deep

Materials

Yardage is based on 42"-wide fabric. Fat eighths measure 9" × 21". In addition to the following materials, you'll need supplies for your favorite appliqué method. Supplies for the Apliquick method used for this project are given on page 7.

7" × 10" rectangle of cream print for appliquéd machine background

1 fat eighth of light beige print for wording background and drawstring pulls

⅝ yard of burgundy yarn-dyed plaid for outer bag and drawstring pulls

⅓ yard of brown stripe for drawstring bag

3" × 4" scrap of gray print for sewing machine

1" × 4" scrap of charcoal print for sewing-machine base

2" × 2" scrap of white print for Mason jar

1" × 2" scrap of gray print for Mason-jar ring

1" × 2" scrap of red print for pincushion top

9 squares, 5" × 5" *each*, of assorted coordinating prints for hexagons

33 precut ¾" paper hexagons *OR* semi-water-soluble appliqué paper hexagons*

12" × 17" piece of thin batting

4 plastic 1" domes for ends of drawstring (Lynette Anderson Designs)

1⅜ yards of cotton cording for drawstring

9½" × 10" piece of fusible embroidery stabilizer, optional

Brown fine-tip fabric marker

Copy paper or template plastic

Water-soluble basting glue, optional

A ¾" hexagon template is provided on page 53 if you prefer to cut your own hexagon papers using lightweight cardstock or appliqué paper.

Embroidery Floss

The colors listed below are for Valdani 6-strand, hand-dyed embroidery floss.

Charcoal (#0126) for Mason-jar ring, pins and needle, scissors, and machine hand wheel

Dark gold (#P5) for random buttons, thread on one spool in mason jar, and daisy centers

Dark red (#078) for thread in machine, heart on end of thread, random buttons, thread on one spool in jar, daisy petals, and fly stitch around drawstring pulls

Green variegated (#0519) for vine and leaves

Light blue (#0578) for dots in sky, thread through scissors, and daisy petals on sewing machine

Light blue variegated (#JP12) for Xs above words; safety pin, random buttons, and thimble in jar; and dashes on sewing-machine base

Light brown (#H212) for tape measure, words, spools and random buttons in jar

Light taupe (#0178) for spool on sewing machine

Pink variegated (#H204) for hearts on sewing machine and wording, birds, and random buttons

Cutting

From the light beige print, cut:
1 rectangle, 3" × 10"
1 square, 6" × 6"

From the burgundy yarn-dyed plaid, cut:
2 rectangles, 4" × 11½"
1 rectangle, 5" × 9½"
2 rectangles, 6½" × 7½"
2 rectangles, 4½" × 7"
1 square, 6" × 6"
60" total of 1½"-wide bias strips

From the brown stripe, cut:
2 rectangles, 10½" × 12"
1 rectangle, 5" × 9½"

From the thin batting, cut:
1 rectangle, 5" × 9½"
2 rectangles, 6½" × 7½"
2 rectangles, 3½" × 4½"

Preparing the Embroidery on the Bag Front

Use ¼" seam allowances. Press seam allowances as indicated by the arrows.

1 With right sides together, sew the cream print and beige print rectangles together to make a rectangle measuring 9½" × 10", including seam allowances.

Make 1 unit,
9½" × 10".

2 Trace the embroidery design on page 51 onto the right side of the pieced rectangle, with the beige print at the bottom, using a brown marker and light source. If using optional fusible embroidery stabilizer, fuse it to the wrong side of the fabric once the tracing is complete.

3 Referring to "Apliquick Method for Turned-Edge Appliqué" on page 7, prepare the sewing machine, sewing-machine base, Mason jar, Mason-jar ring, and pincushion top for turned-edge appliqué using the patterns on page 52. Do *not* cut out the appliqué shapes.

4 Trace the embroidery details on page 51 onto the right side of both appliqué sewing-machine pieces, the Mason jar and ring, and the pincushion piece.

5 Cut out all the traced appliqué pieces ¼" outside the marked perimeter and complete the appliqué shapes using the Apliquick method.

6 Position the sewing-machine appliqué on the pieced rectangle from step 2, referring to the photo on page 43 for placement. Baste in place using pins, thread, or basting glue. Appliqué in place. Repeat for the sewing-machine base, Mason jar and ring, and pincushion.

Embroidering the Rectangle

Referring to the embroidery key on page 51, embroider the designs on the traced rectangle and appliqués using two strands of floss. Once the embroidery is complete, press the work.

Preparing the Drawstring Pulls

1 Trace the drawstring end cover pattern (page 51) onto copy paper or template plastic to make a template. Using the template, trace two circles onto the back of the light beige 6" square and two circles onto the back of the burgundy 6" square. Cut out the circles from the burgundy square, but do *not* cut out the circles from the light beige square.

2 Trace the daisy design on the drawstring end cover pattern onto the right side of the two circles on the light beige squares using a brown marker and light source. Apply fusible embroidery stabilizer to the back of the squares and embroider the designs following the embroidery key on page 51. Cut out the embroidered circles.

3 Thread a hand-sewing needle with a double thread and knot at the end. Work a single row of basting stitches around the perimeter of a circle.

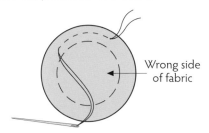

Wrong side of fabric

4 Pull the thread to slightly gather the circle and insert a plastic dome against the wrong side. Continue pulling the thread so that the fabric fits tightly around the dome. Tie off the thread securely. Repeat to cover the remaining three domes using the embroidered and burgundy circles. You will use these in step 8 of "Assembling the Bag" on page 50.

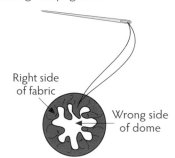

Right side of fabric

Wrong side of dome

Making the Hexagons

1 Referring to "English-Paper-Pieced Hexagons" on page 10 and using the fabric hexagon pattern on page 53, cut 33 hexagons from 8 assorted 5" squares. Glue or thread baste the fabric hexagons to the paper hexagons.

2 Join the hexagons in rows to make a piece that measures approximately 6½" × 7½".

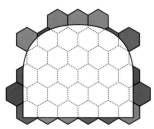

Making the Handles

1 Fold the burgundy 4" × 11½" strips in half lengthwise, wrong sides together; press and open. Fold the cut edges to the pressed line and press. Fold in half and stitch close to both long edges.

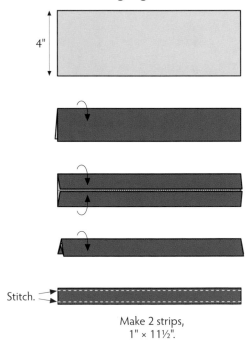

Make 2 strips,
1" × 11½".

2 Stitch approximately ⅛" from the previously stitched lines to finish the handles with a double row of topstitching on each side. Press the raw end of each handle under approximately ¼". Make two handles that measure 1" × 11".

Make 2 handles,
1" × 11".

Preparing the Quilted Outer-Bag Pieces

Use ¼" seam allowances.

1 For the bag base, layer the burgundy, batting, and brown striped 5" × 9½" rectangles. Both fabrics should be right side facing out. Quilt by hand or machine. The bag base shown is machine quilted with parallel diagonal lines.

2 For the bag back, layer the pieced hexagon unit with the 6½" × 7½" batting and burgundy rectangles. Quilt by hand or machine. The bag back is machine quilted in the ditch around each hexagon.

3 Trace the bag front/back and base patterns on pages 52 and 53 to make templates from copy paper.

4 Center the front/back outer-bag template on the prepared bag back piece and cut out. Fold the quilted bag base piece in half, center the bag base template on the fold, and cut out.

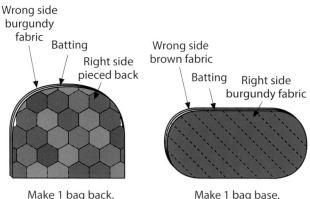

Make 1 bag back.   Make 1 bag base.

5 Layer the embroidered and appliquéd bag front piece with the remaining 6½" × 7½" batting and burgundy rectangles. Center the front/back outer-bag template on the design and cut out. Pin the three layers together and stitch ⅛" from the outer edge to secure; the bag front is not quilted.

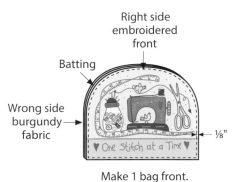

Make 1 bag front.

6 Join the burgundy 1½"-wide bias strips end to end to make a single binding strip. Fold ¼" to the wrong side along the entire length of the strip and press.

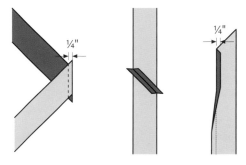

Press seam open.

7 Measure the top curved edge of the bag front and cut a strip of binding ½" longer than this measurement. Matching the raw edges of the bag to the raw edge of the binding, and with right sides facing, sew the strip to the curved edge. Do *not* fold the binding to the wrong side and attach. Repeat for the bag back.

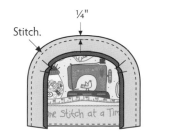

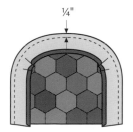

8 Fold a burgundy 4½" × 7" rectangle wrong sides together with the 4½" sides aligned. Insert a batting 3½" × 4½" rectangle inside and quilt by hand with straight lines spaced ½" apart. Repeat to make a second side unit.

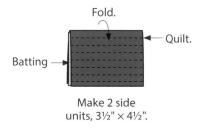

Make 2 side units, 3½" × 4½".

ONE-STITCH-AT-A-TIME SEWING CADDY

Preparing the Inner Drawstring Bag

1 To finish the seams on the inner bag, press under ⅛" twice on all four sides of the brown stripe 10½" × 12" rectangles.

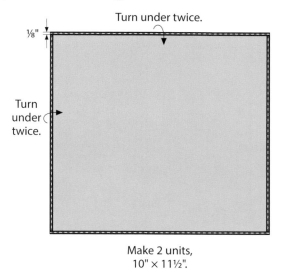

Make 2 units,
10" × 11½".

2 With right sides facing, stitch the brown rectangles together along the finished side seams, leaving a 1" opening for inserting the drawstring 1½" from the top raw edge on each side. Press the side seam allowances open and flat. Topstitch close to the folded edge on both sides of the side seam to neaten the inside seam.

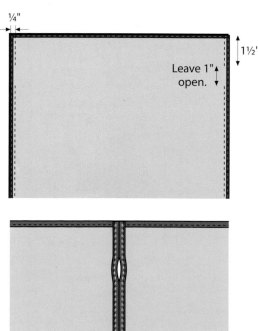

Press open and topstitch.

3 Turn under ½" on the top edge of the drawstring bag and press. Turn under another 1" to create the casing for the drawstring and press. Stitch close to both edges of the 1" turned-down edge. Turn the inner bag right side out.

Assembling the Bag

Use ¼" seam allowances unless otherwise noted.

1 Sew the outer-bag front and back pieces to the side pieces, wrong sides together and with bottom edges aligned. Make sure not to catch the loose edge of the binding in the stitching.

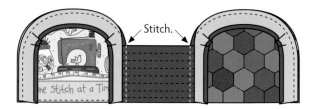

2 Working on one side at a time, fold the binding over the raw edges and hand stitch in place.

Turn binding over edge and hand stitch in place.

3 Use four pins to mark the center of each edge of the bag base. Place a pin at the bottom center of the outer-bag front and back and at the center of each side. Place pins at the center of the drawstring bag front and back.

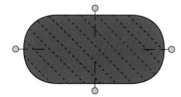

Mark centers with pins.

4 Using the pins to position the pieces, insert and pin the right side of the drawstring bag into the outer bag at the bottom edges. Easing the raw edges in place where necessary, baste around the bottom edge.

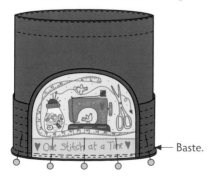

Baste.

5 Again using the centered pins to help with alignment, pin the joined bags from step 4 to the bag base. Generously pin around the entire base. Sew using a scant ¼" seam allowance. Using the remaining prepared bias strip, bind the bag base edges.

Stitch.

Bind.

6 Place the folded ends of the handles against the lining side of the outer bag. Pin them approximately 2½" below the top edge and 3" apart. Hand stitch the handles in place, working stitches to form a square.

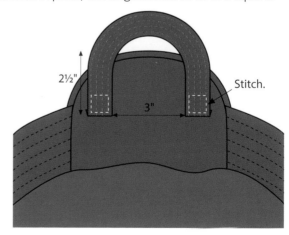

2½"

3"

Stitch.

ONE-STITCH-AT-A-TIME SEWING CADDY

7 Cut two 24"-long pieces of cotton cording. Attaching a safety pin to one end of one length of cording, and starting on the bag left side, thread one length of cording through the drawstring bag casing and back out the left side. Repeat with a second length of cording from the right side.

8 Place the raw edge of the cording on one side of the bag between an embroidered drawstring end cover and a burgundy drawstring end cover. Align the edges around the circumference and join by working a fly stitch completely around the perimeter with two strands of dark red floss. Make sure to catch the cording ends between the two sides of the end cover. Repeat with the two remaining pulls and the opposite cord ends.

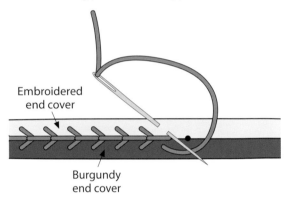

Embroidered
end cover

Burgundy
end cover

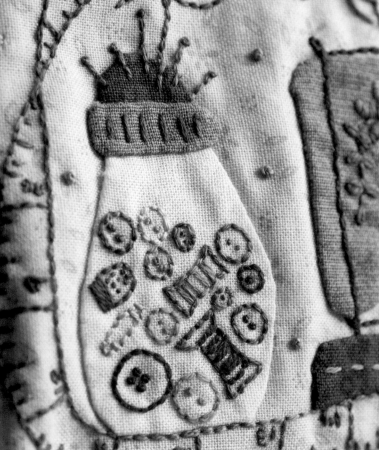

Drawstring End Cover

Embroidery Key

——	Backstitch
✕	Cross-stitch
•	French knot
⌒	Lazy daisy
- - -	Running stitch
■	Satin stitch

Align with seam.

Front template placement

**One-Stitch-at-a-Time Sewing Caddy
Placement and Embroidery Pattern**

Patterns do not include seam allowances and are reversed for Apliquick and fusible appliqué.

Pincushion
Cut 1.

Ring
Cut 1.

Jar
Cut 1.

Sewing machine
Cut 1.

Machine base
Cut 1.

Bag base
Cut 1.

Place on fold.

¼" seam allowance

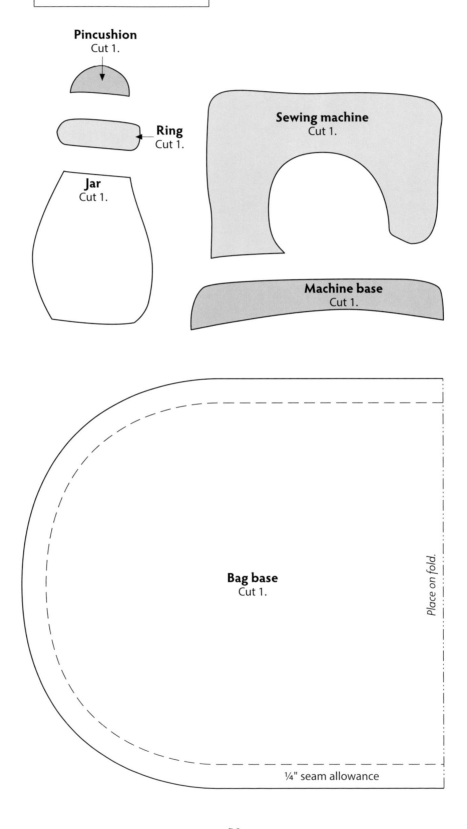

Paper hexagon
Cut 33 from paper.

Fabric hexagon
Cut 33 from fabric.

¼" seam allowance

Outer bag front and back
Cut 1 front from embroidery.
Cut 1 back from patchwork.

¼" seam allowance

Springtime Needle Case and Scissors Holder

It's spring, the birds are busy nesting, the trees and flowers are blooming, and even the cat and dog are at peace! Capture the feeling by making this irresistible needle case in a combination of pretty florals and gorgeous wool. Pair the case with a matching scissors holder to complete the set.

Needle Case

FINISHED SIZE
Approximately 4½" × 6½" (closed)

Materials

Fat eighths measure 9" × 21".

1 fat eighth of cream solid for embroidery background*

1 fat eighth of pink tone on tone for prairie points, inner pocket, and ties

4½" × 42" strip of small-scale floral for heart appliqués and binding

8" × 10" rectangle of large-scale floral for needle-case lining*

Scraps of green tone on tone for prairie points

8" × 14" rectangle of green wool for outer needle case and needle pad

3" × 8" piece of paper-backed fusible web

8" × 18" rectangle of fusible embroidery stabilizer, optional

Brown fine-tip fabric marker

Water-soluble marking pen

Craft glue

If making both the needle case and the scissors holder on page 60, you can cut all the print pieces from 1 fat eighth (9" × 21" piece) of cream solid.

Embroidery Floss

The colors listed are for Cosmo 6-strand embroidery floss.

Black (#600) for cat, dog collar, string holding birdhouse, birds' and dog's eyes, line under first alphabet row, centers of two-petal flowers, and dashed line below two-petal flowers

Cream (#364) for pocket dividers, needle-pad stitching

Dark chocolate (#4311) for tree trunk and branches, birdhouse, birds, dashed lines above and below daisies on needle case front, and dashed line on needle case pocket

Dusky pink (#654) for daisies and birds' wings

Gold (#575) for dog, birds' legs and beaks, dots before and after year, X after name, and two-petal flowers

Medium eggplant (#763) for birdhouse roof, outer dashed and solid lines, nine-patch grid, line above first alphabet row, line above two-petal flowers, and name

Olive green (#685) stems, leaves, alphabet, cats' eyes, nine-patch dots, pocket wording

Rose (#655) for daisy centers, heart, heart string, line below year and name, and cats' noses and mouths

Cutting

From the cream solid, cut:
1 rectangle, 7" × 9"
1 rectangle, 6" × 8"

From the pink tone on tone, cut:
1 strip, 1¼" × 20"
1 rectangle, 5½" × 9½"
5 squares, 1" × 1"

From the green tone on tone, cut:
5 squares, 1" × 1"

From the small-scale floral, cut:
1 strip, 1¼" × 42"
1 rectangle, 3" × 5"

From the large-scale floral, cut:
1 rectangle, 6½" × 9½"

From the green wool, cut:
1 rectangle, 6½" × 9½"
1 rectangle, 2¼" × 3¼"

Embroidering the Rectangles

1 Trace the needle case front and pocket embroidery patterns on page 59 onto the right sides of the large and small cream rectangles using the brown marker and a light source. If using optional fusible embroidery stabilizer, cut a 7" × 9" rectangle and a 6" × 8" rectangle and fuse them to the wrong side of the corresponding cream rectangles once the tracing is complete.

2 Referring to the embroidery key on page 59, work all the embroidery in the floss colors listed, noting the stitches used. Use one strand of floss for the dog's collar, strings, animal faces, leaves, alphabet, dots, daisies, and name; use two strands for all other design elements. Add your name and the date to the large rectangle, referring to the photo on page 55 for placement and using the alphabet and number patterns on page 59.

3 Once you've completed the embroidery, press each rectangle well. Trim the large rectangle to 4½" × 6" and the small rectangle to 2¾" × 4¾", centering each design.

Preparing the Prairie Points and Pocket

1 Press a pink or green tone-on-tone 1" square in half so that the fold is at the top. One at a time, fold the top corners down to meet at the bottom center as shown and press. Glue baste the folds to secure if desired. Repeat to make 10 prairie points, 5 of each color.

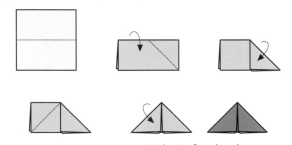

Make 5 of each color.

2 Fold the pink 5½" × 9½" rectangle in half lengthwise, with the fold at the top. With the water-soluble marking pen, mark the vertical center of the rectangle. Then measure and mark three equal sections on the

left-hand side, making sure to account for the ¼" seam allowance on the left side.

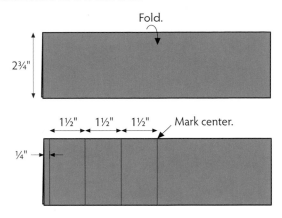

Appliquéing Patches and Hearts

1 Referring to "Fusible Appliqué" on page 10 and using the pattern on page 59, trace three hearts onto the paper side of the fusible web, leaving at least ½" between hearts. Cut approximately ¼" outside the marked lines.

2 Fuse the heart shapes to the wrong side of the small-scale floral rectangle. Cut out each heart accurately on the lines, and once cool, peel off the paper backing.

3 Position a heart in the center of each of the three sections marked on the left side of the pocket, ½" from the bottom. Press in place. Using two strands of embroidery floss, blanket-stitch around each heart as shown.

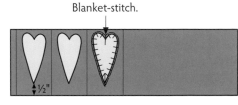

Appliqué placement

4 Fold under the edges of the small embroidered rectangle approximately ⅛" from the embroidered frame line. Pin or glue baste the rectangle to the right

half of the pocket piece, ½" from the bottom and side edges. Appliqué the prepared rectangle to the pocket.

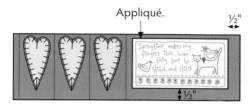

Appliqué placement

5 Press the green wool 6½" × 9½" rectangle in half vertically to crease. Fold under the edges of the large embroidered rectangle approximately ⅛" from the embroidered frame line. Center and pin or glue baste the embroidered rectangle to the right half of the wool rectangle.

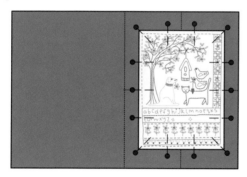

Appliqué placement

6 Place five prairie points beneath the top edge of the front embroidered rectangle as shown, with colors alternating and with each one slightly overlapping the next; pin or glue baste. Repeat with the remaining five prairie points at the bottom edge of the rectangle. Appliqué the rectangle to the wool background, making sure to stitch through the prairie points.

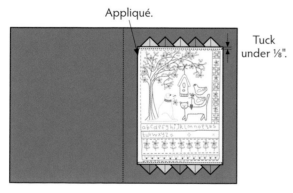

Tuck under ⅛".

Finishing the Needle Case

For more detailed information about any finishing steps, visit ShopMartingale.com/HowtoQuilt.

1 Position the embellished pocket piece on the bottom of the floral 6½" × 9½" lining rectangle with the raw edges aligned; pin in place. Work a running stitch with two strands of cream floss on the marked section lines to divide the pocket.

2 Position and pin the wool 2¼" × 3¼" rectangle on the upper-left quadrant of the lining rectangle as shown. Using two strands of cream floss, blanket-stitch around the edge of the wool rectangle to attach. Refer to "Embroidery Stitch Guide" on page 12 for guidance.

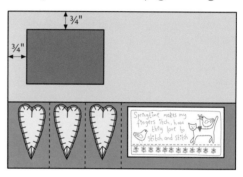

Appliqué placement

3 To make the ties, fold the pink tone-on-tone 1¼"-wide strip in half lengthwise and finger-press to crease. Open out and fold the long raw edges inward, wrong sides facing, to meet at the crease line; press. Fold in half again and press. Topstitch close to both long edges. Cut the strip into two 9½"-long tie pieces.

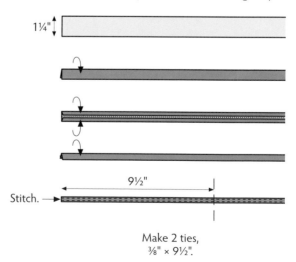

Make 2 ties, ⅜" × 9½".

4 Place the prepared needle case front and lining wrong sides together. On the lining side (case interior), pin one tie at the center of each side edge as shown, with the ties facing inward. Finish the case edges with a single-fold binding, using the floral 1¼"-wide strip. Machine stitch it to the case front (wool side) and slipstitch it to the case interior, catching the ends of the ties in the binding.

Wrong side of needle case front

Right side of needle case lining

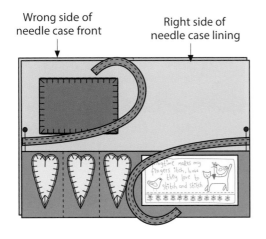

Slip-stitch binding to inside.

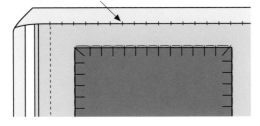

Pattern does not include seam allowances and is reversed for fusible appliqué.

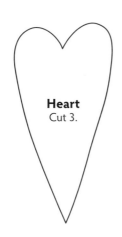

Heart
Cut 3.

Needle Case Front Embroidery Pattern

Needle Case Pocket Embroidery Pattern

0123456789

Needle Case Number Embroidery Pattern

Embroidery Key

— Backstitch

X Cross-stitch

• French knot

⌒ Lazy daisy

– – Running stitch

■ Satin stitch

SPRINGTIME NEEDLE CASE AND SCISSORS HOLDER

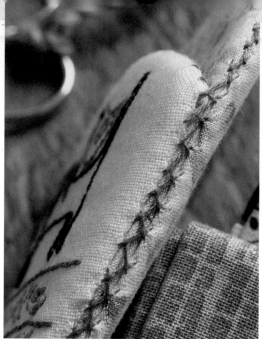

Scissors Holder

FINISHED SIZE
2⅜" × 4⅛"

Materials

6" × 6" square of cream solid for embroidery background*

5" × 10" rectangle of small-scale floral for holder front and back

10" × 10" square of medium-weight cardstock

10" × 10" square of thin batting

6" × 6" square of fusible embroidery stabilizer, optional

Brown fine-tip fabric marker

Craft glue

If making both the scissors holder and the needle case on page 54, you can cut all pieces from 1 fat eighth of cream solid.

Embroidery Floss

The colors listed below are for Cosmo 6-strand embroidery floss.

Black (#600) for cat, bird's eye, and centers of two-petal flowers

Dark chocolate (#4311) for lines above and below daisies

Dusky pink (#654) for daisies, bird, dashed line below two-petal flowers, and stitching around holder

Gold (#575) for bird's feet and beak, two-petal flowers, and dots before and after name

Medium eggplant (#763) for line above and below name

Olive green (#685) for stems, leaves, line between dashes, cat's eyes, name, twisted cord, and tassel

Rose (#655) for daisy centers, heart, heart string, cat's nose and mouth, twisted cord, and tassel

Embroidering the Square

1 Trace the scissors holder embroidery pattern on page 62 onto the right side of the cream 6" square using a brown marker and light source. If using optional fusible embroidery stabilizer, fuse it to the wrong side of the fabric square once the tracing is complete.

2 Referring to the embroidery key on page 62, work all the embroidery in the floss colors listed, noting the stitches used. Use one strand of floss for the two-petal flowers, dashed line, daisies, string, and cat's face; use two strands for all other design elements. Add your name, referring to the photo on page 60 for placement and using the alphabet on page 62.

3 Once you've completed the embroidery, press the square well.

Making the Scissors Holder

1 Using the scissors holder patterns on page 63, trace and cut out the pieces from cardstock, batting, floral print, and the embroidered piece as indicated on the patterns. To cut the embroidered piece, place the pattern on the wrong side of the embroidered square. Hold it up to the light to check that the embroidery is positioned correctly and cut it out.

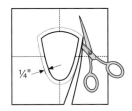

¼"

2 Center the pocket and base cardstock pieces on the corresponding batting pieces and glue in place.

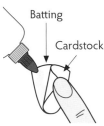

Batting

Cardstock

Make 2 pocket units.

Batting

Cardstock

Make 2 base units.

3 Place the batting side of the cardstock base against the wrong side of a floral base piece. Glue around the edge on the cardstock and fold the ¼" seam allowances of the fabric over the edge onto the glue.

Finger-press until the glue sets. Repeat to make a second base piece, a floral pocket piece, and an embroidered pocket piece.

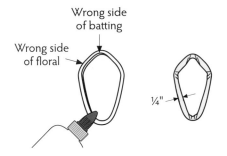

Wrong side of batting

Wrong side of floral

¼"

Make 2 floral base pieces.

Make 1 floral pocket piece.

Make 1 embroidered pocket piece.

Making the Tassel and Cord

1 To make the tassel, cut out a 1¼" × 3" rectangle from cardstock. Using all six strands, wrap approximately 30" of both olive green and rose floss around the 1¼" width 10 times. Start counting wraps from the bottom of the card. When you have reached the desired tassel size, carefully slide the loops off the card.

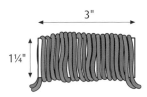

3"

1¼"

2 Twist 48" of both the pink and green flosses together until the cord you're creating almost doubles back on itself, but don't let it double back yet.

3 Thread the twisted cord through the top loop of the tassel, center the tassel on the cord, and let the cord double back on itself. Hold onto the ends while it twists. Tie a small knot at the end to secure the twisted cord. Cut through the bottom loops of the tassel. Wrap another length of floss around the tassel approximately ¼" from the top loop. Secure with a knot and tuck the thread ends out of sight.

Finishing the Scissors Holder

1 Glue the two pocket pieces wrong sides together. Hold while the glue is drying or use a clothespin.

2 Glue the two base pieces wrong sides together, sandwiching the ends of the twisted cord at the center top between the two pieces.

3 With two strands of dusky pink embroidery floss, work a herringbone stitch across the seam of the pocket's top edge to secure the layers together. Place the pocket and base wrong sides together, aligning the pieces at the sides and around the bottom edge. Stitch around the edge using a herringbone stitch.

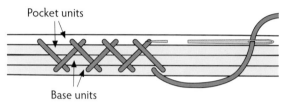

Pocket units

Base units

Pocket template placement

Scissors Holder Embroidery Pattern

Embroidery Key

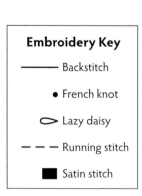

——— Backstitch

• French knot

⬭ Lazy daisy

– – – Running stitch

■ Satin stitch

ABCDEFGHIJKLMNOPQRSTUVWXYZ

abcdefghijklmnopqrstuvwxyz

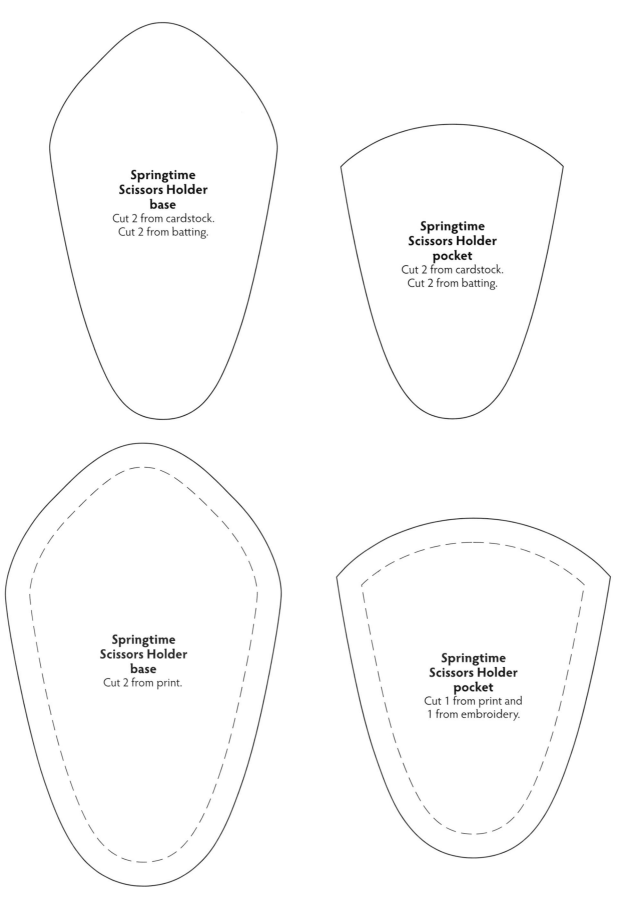

**Springtime
Scissors Holder
base**
Cut 2 from cardstock.
Cut 2 from batting.

**Springtime
Scissors Holder
pocket**
Cut 2 from cardstock.
Cut 2 from batting.

**Springtime
Scissors Holder
base**
Cut 2 from print.

**Springtime
Scissors Holder
pocket**
Cut 1 from print and
1 from embroidery.

SPRINGTIME NEEDLE CASE AND SCISSORS HOLDER

Count Your Blessings Mini-Quilt

Making a sampler-style wall quilt gives you a great opportunity to hone your favorite stitches. Combine the embroidery with turned-edge appliqué and a bit of piecing to take advantage of all your skills in one pretty little project. Add a hand-painted button or two for a touch of novelty and dimension.

FINISHED SIZE
9½" × 14"

Materials

In addition to the following materials, you'll need supplies for your favorite appliqué method. Supplies for the Apliquick method used for this project are given on page 7.

8" × 11" rectangle of cream print for embroidery background

12 strips, 1¼" × 14" *each,* of assorted coordinating prints

1½" × 3" rectangle of purple print for roof

1½" × 5" rectangle of green print for hill

2½" × 3" rectangle of gray print for house

1½" × 1½" square of light blue print for front door

⅛ yard of blue check for single-fold binding

14" × 18" rectangle of coordinating print for backing

14" × 18" rectangle of lightweight batting

¼" × ¾" moon button (YB370 Crescent Moon from Lynette Anderson Designs)

8" × 11" rectangle of fusible embroidery stabilizer, optional

Brown fine-tip fabric marker

Water-soluble basting glue, optional

Embroidery Floss

The colors listed below are for Cosmo 6-strand embroidery floss.

Charcoal (#895) for partial alphabet, windows, date, and dots following alphabet

Country blue (#734) for bird, bird's wing, small stars, frame outline, and letters c and w

Dark green (#637) for pine needles, daisy leaves, and lines above and below Xs

Dark red (#246) for large heart, chimneys, and numbers

Eggplant (#765) for daisy centers, large star on tree, and letter r

Light brown (#369) for trees and daisy stems

Light pink (#235) for words, Xs above daisies, and letter p

Medium eggplant (#763) for daisy petals, small heart on door, Xs below daisies, and letter m

Cutting

From the assorted coordinating prints, cut:

1 strip, 1¼" × 9½" (piece 1)
1 strip, 1¼" × 5¾" (piece 2)
1 strip, 1¼" × 10¼" (piece 3)
1 strip, 1¼" × 6½" (piece 4)
1 strip, 1¼" × 11" (piece 5)
1 strip, 1¼" × 7¼" (piece 6)
1 strip, 1¼" × 11¾" (piece 7)
1 strip, 1¼" × 8" (piece 8)
1 strip, 1¼" × 12½" (piece 9)
1 strip, 1¼" × 8¾" (piece 10)
1 strip, 1¼" × 13¼" (piece 11)
1 strip, 1¼" × 9½" (piece 12)

From the blue check, cut:

2 strips, 1½" × 42"

Preparing the Background

1 Referring to "Apliquick Method for Turned-Edge Appliqué" on page 7, prepare the roof, house, hill, and door using appliqué paper and the patterns on page 67. Do *not* cut out the appliqué shapes.

2 Trace the embroidery designs onto the right side of the house and door shapes using a brown marker and light source. Trace the desired date, using the number patterns provided, or use your own printing. Refer to "Transferring Embroidery Designs" on page 11 for additional information.

3 Cut out all the appliqué shapes ¼" outside the marked perimeter and complete the appliqué using the Apliquick method.

4 Using the placement and embroidery pattern on page 68, trace the embroidery design onto the cream rectangle using the brown marker and a light source.

5 Position the house on the traced cream rectangle and baste it in place using pins, thread, or basting glue. Refer to the pattern on page 68 for placement. Appliqué in place. Position, baste, and appliqué the roof and door.

6 If using optional fusible embroidery stabilizer, fuse it to the wrong side of the appliquéd rectangle.

Embroidering the Rectangle

1 Referring to the embroidery key on page 68, complete all the embroidery. Use one strand of floss for the small stars; use two strands for all other design elements. Once the embroidery is complete, press the work.

2 Trim the embroidered rectangle to 5" × 9½", centering the design.

Making the Log-Cabin Border

Use ¼" seam allowances. Press seam allowances toward the piece just added.

1 Join pieces 1–4 in numerical order, beginning on the right side of the embroidered rectangle and working clockwise. The unit should measure 6½" × 11", including seam allowances.

Make 1 unit,
6½" × 11".

2 Join pieces 5–8 in the same manner. The unit should now measure 8" × 12½", including seam allowances.

3 Join the remaining pieces in the same manner. The finished mini-quilt top should measure 9½" × 14".

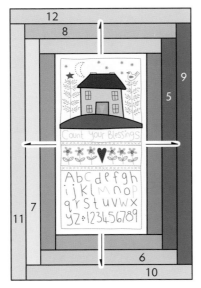

Make 1 unit,
9½" × 14".

Finishing the Quilt

For more detailed information about any finishing steps, visit ShopMartingale.com/HowtoQuilt.

1 Layer the quilt top, backing, and batting; baste the layers together. Quilt by hand or machine. The quilt shown is machine quilted in the ditch of the log-cabin border.

2 Join the two blue check 1½"-wide strips end to end to make one long strip and use it to finish the quilt with a single-fold binding.

3 Sew on the moon button, referring to the pattern for placement.

Patterns do not include seam allowances and are reversed for Apliquick and fusible appliqué.

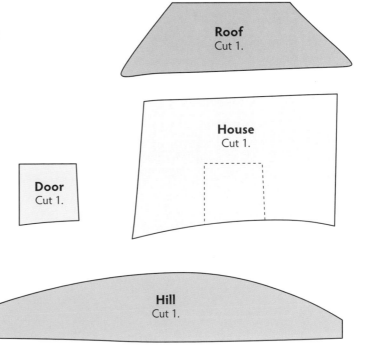

Roof
Cut 1.

House
Cut 1.

Door
Cut 1.

Hill
Cut 1.

Button placement

0123456789

Count Your Blessings

Fill with French knots.

A B C d e f g h
i j k l M N o P
q r S t u v w X
Y Z : 1 2 3 4 5 6 7 8 9

Count Your Blessings Mini-Quilt Placement and Embroidery Pattern

Embroidery Key

——	Backstitch
✕	Cross-stitch
•	French knot
– – –	Running stitch
■	Satin stitch
✳	Star stitch
—	Straight stitch

Four Seasons Wall Hanging

A special little cottage makes for a picturesque scene any season of the year. Embroider all four designs and group them together in a lovely wall hanging— or pick your favorite to give a decorative pillow your personal touch.

FINISHED SIZE
27" × 24"

FREE PILLOW PATTERN ONLINE!

Download a matching pillow pattern at ShopMartingale.com/LynettesBestLovedStitcheries!

Materials

Yardage is based on 42"-wide fabric. In addition to the following materials, you'll need supplies for your favorite appliqué method. Supplies for the Apliquick method used for this project are given on page 7.

¼ yard of cream print for embroidery backgrounds

¾ yard of blue solid for block frames, center square, border, and binding

⅝ yard *total* of 15 assorted coordinating prints for patchwork background

9" × 9" square of medium blue print for roofs and watermelon rind

9" × 9" square of light blue print for houses

4" × 4" square of purple print for house doors

3" × 3" square of ecru print for beehive

3" × 3" square of blue print for beehive door and snowman hat

3" × 3" square of rose print for watermelon

3" × 3" square of gray print for pumpkins

4" × 4" square of white print for snowman and snow on roof

⅞ yard of coordinating print for backing

28" × 31" piece of batting

¼ yard of fusible embroidery stabilizer, optional

Brown fine-tip fabric marker

Embroidery Floss

The colors listed below are for Cosmo 6-strand embroidery floss.

Blue (#982) for daisies; stars; snowman's scarf; and box around words *Spring, Summer, Autumn,* and *Winter*

Charcoal (#895) for bees; bees' flight paths; dashes on beehive; birds' eyes; strings; windows; roof detail; letters and numbers; words *Spring, Summer, Autumn,* and *Winter;* peacock's body; boxes around hearts; watermelon seeds; crows; lines on pumpkins; fox's eye; and snowman's eyes, hat brim, buttons, and mitten string

Dark brown (#312) for trees, beehive stand, snowman's arms, fox, and sled

Dark green (#925) for border lines, field line, chimney, birdhouse, daisy stems and leaves, tree leaves, peacock's tail feathers, and pumpkin vines

Gold (#575) for birds' beaks and legs, bees, peacock's beak and legs, strawberry seeds, sun, crows' beaks, tree leaves, berries on wreath, and star

Mauve (#236) for buds in field and on tree, hearts, birdhouse roof, all Xs, dashes in border, strawberries, dots in field, snowman's scarf, and birds' breasts

Medium green (#924) for field, flower stems, tree leaves, strawberry stems and tops, wreath, snowman's mittens, pine needles, and leaves on buds and daisies

Tan (#368) for fence, dashes below field line, birds, pumpkin stalks, snowman's nose, and chimney smoke

White (#100) for daisy centers, dots in sky, moon, crows' eyes, snowflakes, snow on fence posts, buds in field, window ledges, and fox's tail

Cutting

From the cream print, cut:
4 rectangles, 8" × 9"

From the blue solid, cut:
3 strips, 1½" × 42"
2 strips, 2½" × 27"
2 strips, 2½" × 20"
8 strips, 1½" × 6½"
8 strips, 1¼" × 9½"
1 square, 2" × 2"

From *each* of the 15 assorted coordinating prints, cut:
5 squares, 2¾" × 2¾" (75 total; 1 will be extra)

From the fusible embroidery stabilizer (optional), cut:
4 rectangles, 8" × 9"

Preparing the Background

1 Referring to "Apliquick Method for Turned-Edge Appliqué" on page 7, prepare the house, roof, house door, beehive and beehive door, watermelon and watermelon rind, pumpkins, snow, snowman, and snowman's hat using the patterns on page 75. You will make four houses, four roofs, four house doors, and one each of the remaining shapes from the appropriate fabrics. Do *not* cut out the appliqué shapes yet.

2 Trace the embroidery details onto the right side of the houses, roofs, doors, beehive, watermelon, pumpkins, and snowman shapes using a brown marker and light source. Note that some details extend off the appliqué shapes; these may need to be added with a touch of freehand drawing.

3 Cut out all the appliqués ¼" outside the marked perimeter and complete the appliqués using the Apliquick method.

4 Using the placement and embroidery patterns on pages 76–79, center and trace each embroidery design onto a cream rectangle.

5 Working with one traced pattern at a time, position the house appliqué, referring to the embroidery pattern for placement. Baste it in place using pins, thread, or basting glue. Appliqué in place. Position, baste, and appliqué the remaining shapes, slightly overlapping the edges and layering the pieces as indicated. Apply the corresponding appliqués to all four rectangles.

6 If using optional fusible embroidery stabilizer, fuse a piece to the wrong side of each appliquéd rectangle.

Embroidering the Rectangles

1 Referring to the embroidery key given with each design, embroider each scene, including the appliqué details. Use one strand of floss for the small bees' stripes, strings, tree markings, birdhouse, watermelon seeds, pumpkin lines, stars, tree details, chimney, and wreath; use two strands for all other design elements.

2 Once the embroidery is complete, press. Trim each embroidered rectangle to 6½" × 7½", making sure to center the designs.

Framing the Embroidered Blocks

Use ¼" seam allowances. Press seam allowances as indicated by the arrows.

Stitch blue 1½" × 6½" strips to the sides of the finished spring embroidery. Stitch blue 1¼" × 9½" strips to the top and bottom to complete the frame around the embroidery, which should measure 9½" × 8", including seam allowances. Repeat to frame the remaining three embroidered scenes.

Make 4 framed blocks,
9½" × 8".

TINY FUSES

For tiny appliqués, such as doors and hats, you might prefer to use the "Fusible Appliqué" technique on page 10.

Making the Quilt Center

1 Using a pencil, draw a line diagonally from corner to corner on the wrong side of 37 assorted squares.

2 Place a marked square right sides together with an unmarked square of a different print. Stitch ¼" from each side of the drawn line. Carefully cut on the marked line to make a half-square-triangle unit; press open. Make 74 units measuring 2⅜" square, including seam allowances.

Make 74 units,
2⅜" × 2⅜".

3 Organize the half-square-triangle units into pairs of different fabric combinations. On the wrong side of one unit from each pair, draw a line diagonally from corner to corner, intersecting the seam allowance. Place the marked unit right sides together with the unmarked unit, aligning the seams. Stitch ¼" from each side of the drawn line. Carefully cut on the marked line to make an hourglass unit; press open. Make 74 hourglass units measuring 2" square, including seam allowances.

Make 74 units,
2" × 2".

Assembling the Wall Hanging

1 Arrange 10 hourglass units in two groups of five and join to make two sashing strips measuring 2" × 8", including seam allowances.

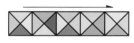

Make 2 strips,
2" × 8".

2 Lay out the Spring block next to the Summer block, with a sashing strip between them. Join the pieces. Repeat to join the Autumn and Winter blocks with the second sashing strip. The units should measure 8" × 20", including seam allowances.

Make 2 units,
8" × 20".

FOUR SEASONS WALL HANGING

center patchwork row. Join patchwork borders to the sides of the unit. Complete the wall-hanging center by adding the top and bottom patchwork borders. The wall-hanging center should measure 20" × 23", including seam allowances.

5 Sew blue 2½" × 20" strips to the sides of the wall-hanging center. Sew blue 2½" × 27" strips to the top and bottom to complete the outer border. The wall hanging should now measure 27" × 24", including seam allowances.

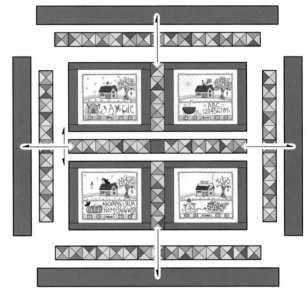

Wall-hanging assembly

Finishing the Wall Hanging

For more detailed information about any finishing steps, including adding a hanging sleeve, visit ShopMartingale.com/HowtoQuilt.

1 Layer the wall hanging, batting, and backing; baste the layers together. Quilt by hand or machine. The wall hanging shown is machine quilted in the ditch of the blue border and the embroidered panels, and horizontally across the center of each embroidered panel with straight-line quilting. All the hourglass rows are quilted with a bud, heart, leaf, and swirl design.

2 Trim the backing and batting even with the wall-hanging front. Join the blue 1½"-wide strips end to end to make one long strip and use it to bind the wall-hanging edges with single-fold binding.

3 Arrange 12 hourglass units in a row with the blue 2" square in the center and join to make the center patchwork row, which should measure 2" × 20", including seam allowances. Make two rows of 11 hourglass units for the side patchwork borders, which should measure 2" × 17", including seam allowances. Repeat to make two rows of 15 hourglass units for the top and bottom borders, which should measure 2" × 23", including seam allowances.

Make 1 row,
2" × 20".

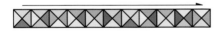

Make 2 rows,
2" × 17".

Make 2 rows,
2" × 23".

4 Referring to the wall-hanging assembly diagram, join the embroidered units to the top and bottom of the

Patterns do not include seam allowances and are reversed for Apliquick and fusible appliqué.

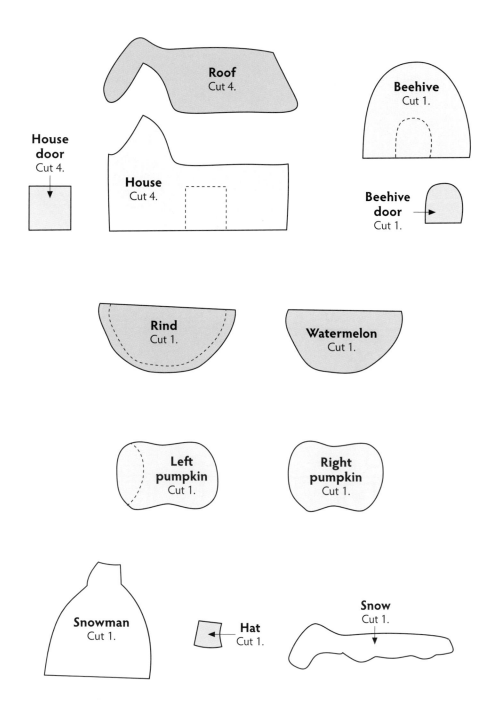

Roof
Cut 4.

House door
Cut 4.

House
Cut 4.

Beehive
Cut 1.

Beehive door
Cut 1.

Rind
Cut 1.

Watermelon
Cut 1.

Left pumpkin
Cut 1.

Right pumpkin
Cut 1.

Snowman
Cut 1.

Hat
Cut 1.

Snow
Cut 1.

Four Seasons Wall Hanging: Spring

Embroidery Key

—— Backstitch	◯ Lazy daisy
✕ Cross-stitch	– – – Running stitch
• French knot	◼ Satin stitch

Four Seasons Wall Hanging: Summer

Embroidery Key

—— Backstitch	◌ Lazy daisy
✕ Cross-stitch	– – – Running stitch
• French knot	◼ Satin stitch

Long & short stitch

Four Seasons Wall Hanging: Autumn

Embroidery Key

—— Backstitch	– – – Long & short stitch
✕ Cross-stitch	– – Running stitch
● French knot	▮ Satin stitch
⟃ Lazy daisy	

Four Seasons Wall Hanging: Winter

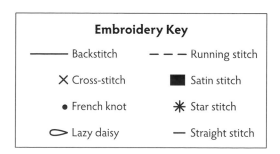

Embroidery Key

——	Backstitch	– – –	Running stitch
✗	Cross-stitch	■	Satin stitch
•	French knot	✳	Star stitch
⬭	Lazy daisy	—	Straight stitch

The Potting Shed Journal Cover and Pencil Case

A fabric-covered journal decorated with charming stitchery is ideal for recording your thoughts and memories. If you sketch designs or scribble recipe ideas as I do, make sure you keep the companion pencil case nearby. Wool flowers bring a three-dimensional touch to the embroidery and appliqué, and the novelty of a beautiful hand-painted wooden button completes the look.

Journal

FINISHED SIZE
Approximately 6¾" × 8¾" (closed)

Materials

In addition to the following materials, you'll need supplies for your favorite appliqué method. Supplies for the Apliquick method used for this project are given on page 7.

8" × 10" rectangle of cream solid for oval embroidery background*

2½" × 5" scrap of tan solid for potting shed

1½" × 2½" scrap of red print for potting shed roof*

10" × 20" rectangle of tan floral for journal cover

10" × 20" rectangle of oatmeal solid for journal-cover lining

2" × 2" scrap of tan wool for flowers

2" × 3" scrap of red wool for flowers, watering can, and beehive door*

10" × 20" rectangle of lightweight fusible interfacing for journal cover

Paper-backed fusible web

¾" × ⅝" bird button (YB006 Erin's Bird from Lynette Anderson Designs)

8" × 10" rectangle of fusible embroidery stabilizer, optional

6⅜" × 8¼" journal or notepad**

Cardstock or template plastic

Brown fine-tip fabric marker

Water-soluble fabric-glue pen, optional

Water-soluble basting glue, optional

*If making both the journal cover and the pencil case on page 87, you can cut both ovals from 1 fat eighth (9" × 21" piece) of cream solid. Omit the red fabric for the shed's roof and cut it from the pencil case's leftover hexagon fabric. Omit the red rectangle of wool and use leftovers from the pencil case's red oval.

**If you want to use a journal of a different size, adjust the dimensions of the cover to fit, remembering that you may need to adjust the fabric requirements. Make sure the journal is at least 6¼" wide and 6½" long so that the embroidery and appliqué will fit.

Embroidery Floss

The colors listed below are for Cosmo 6-strand embroidery floss.

Dark brown (#312) for flowering vine

Country red (#2241) for sun, bee and flight path, beehive, rooflines, window, door and sign, pitchfork, flowerpot, flowers, watering-can handles, ground, grass and buds, and details on taupe wool flowers and beehive door

Taupe (#367) for heart and base on watering can, doorknob on beehive door, and details on red wool flowers

Cutting

From the oatmeal solid, cut:
1 rectangle, 9½" × 18½"

From the lightweight fusible interfacing, cut:
1 rectangle, 9¼" × 18¼"

Preparing the Background

1 Referring to "Apliquick Method for Turned-Edge Appliqué" on page 7, prepare the shed, roof, and oval shapes for turned-edge appliqué using the patterns on page 85. Do *not* cut out the appliqué shapes.

2 Using the placement and embroidery pattern on page 85, trace the embroidery details for the shed and roof onto the right side of the prepared shapes using a brown marker and light source. Refer to "Transferring Embroidery Designs" on page 11 for additional information.

3 Cut out the shed and roof a scant ¼" outside the marked perimeter and complete the appliqué shapes using the Apliquick method.

4 Using the placement and embroidery pattern, trace the oval outline onto the wrong side of the cream rectangle, keeping it centered. Turn the rectangle to the right side and trace the embroidery design, centering it in the oval.

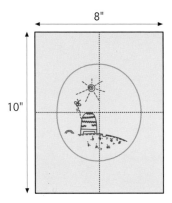

Embroidery placement

5 Position the shed appliqué on the cream solid, referring to the pattern on page 85 for placement. Baste it in place using pins, thread, or basting glue. Appliqué in place. Position, baste, and appliqué the roof.

6 If using optional fusible embroidery stabilizer, fuse it to the wrong side of the appliquéd rectangle.

Embroidering the Oval

Referring to the embroidery key on page 85, embroider the beehive, bee, sun, shed, shed roof, flowerpot, pitchfork, ground details, and top handle of the watering can onto the oval using two strands of floss. Once the embroidery is complete, press the work.

Preparing the Oval

1 Cut out the embroidered oval on the marked line. With the wrong side up, fold the ¼" seam allowance toward the wrong side, basting in place as you go. Press gently.

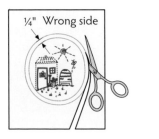 

2 Place the tan floral 10" × 20" rectangle right side up on a flat surface. Place the oval 2¼" from the top and bottom and 4⅛" from the right edge. Baste in place using pins, thread, or basting glue. Appliqué in place.

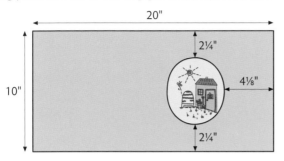

20"

2¼"

4⅛"

10"

2¼"

Appliqué placement

3 Referring to the pattern on page 86 and using a brown marker and a light box, trace the vine around the oval.

4 Referring to the embroidery key on page 86, embroider the vine using two strands of dark brown floss.

Appliquéing the Wool

1 Referring to "Fusible Appliqué" on page 10 and using the reversed patterns on page 85, trace the watering can, beehive door, and flowers onto the paper side of the fusible web the number of times indicated. Cut out the shapes ¼" outside the traced lines.

2 Following the manufacturer's instructions, fuse 11 flowers to the tan wool. Fuse 15 flowers, the watering can, and the beehive door to the red wool. Cut out each shape on the marked line.

3 Referring to the flower placement and vine embroidery pattern on page 86, position and fuse the shapes to the right side of the appliquéd floral rectangle.

4 Using red floss, blanket-stitch around the beehive door and watering can. Backstitch the side handle of the watering can. Using taupe floss, work a French knot for the beehive doorknob, a satin stitch for the watering-can heart, and a running stitch for the watering-can base.

5 Embroider three French knots at the center and whipstitch around the edges of each flower, using red floss for the taupe flowers and taupe floss for the red flowers.

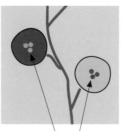

Make 3 French knots on flowers.

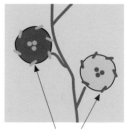

Take little stitches at the edge of each flower.

THE POTTING SHED JOURNAL COVER AND PENCIL CASE

6 Trim the embellished floral rectangle to 9½" × 18½", keeping the oval 2" from the top and bottom edges and 3⅜" from the right edge.

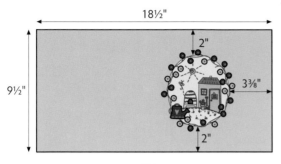

Trim.

7 Following the manufacturer's instructions, center and fuse the lightweight fusible interfacing to the wrong side of the embellished rectangle.

Making the Journal Cover

1 Place the fused fabric and oatmeal lining right sides together, aligning the edges. Backstitching at the beginning and end to secure, stitch around the edge using a ¼" seam allowance, leaving a 3"-wide opening about 2" from a lower corner. Clip all four corners to reduce bulk.

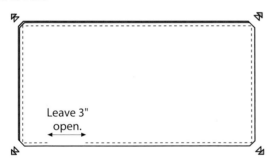

Leave 3" open.

2 Turn the journal cover right side out through the opening. Carefully push out the corners. Press lightly, making sure that none of the lining fabric can be seen from the front.

POINT PUSHERS

You can use any number of pointed objects to gently push out the corners. If you don't have a point-turner tool, try a bamboo stick, a dull pencil, a pointed wine stopper, or the end of a dowel stick that you've sharpened with a pencil sharpener. Just make sure that whatever you use isn't too sharply pointed.

3 Lay the journal cover on a flat work surface, wrong side up. Center the opened journal on the cover. Fold the fabric over the front and back covers to form sleeves, and then close the journal to ensure that the folds allow for the depth of the spine. Pin the folds in place along the top and bottom edges. (My folds measured 2⅛" wide, but depending on the depth of your journal, yours may differ.) Remove the journal from the cover and stitch through all layers of the flaps, close to the top and bottom of the journal, to form the sleeves.

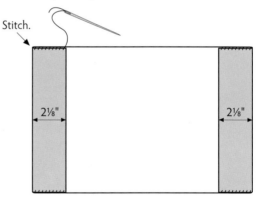

Stitch.

4 Sew the bird button to the roof of the potting shed with red floss and then slip the cover onto the journal.

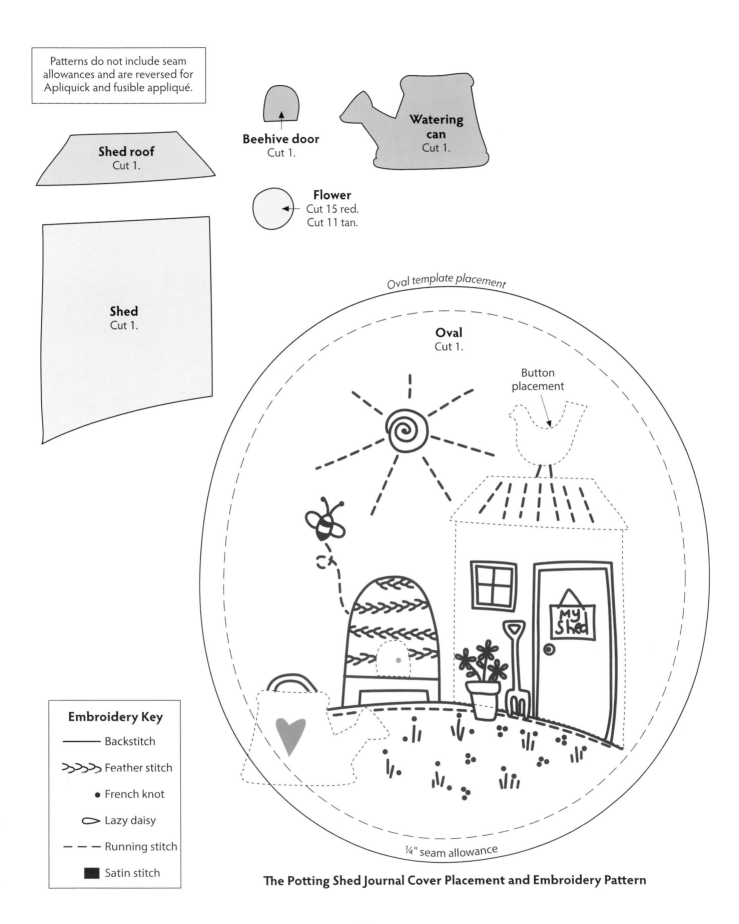

Patterns do not include seam allowances and are reversed for Apliquick and fusible appliqué.

Shed roof
Cut 1.

Shed
Cut 1.

Beehive door
Cut 1.

Watering can
Cut 1.

Flower
Cut 15 red.
Cut 11 tan.

Oval template placement

Oval
Cut 1.

Button placement

My Shed

¼" seam allowance

Embroidery Key

— Backstitch

>>>> Feather stitch

• French knot

⬯ Lazy daisy

- - - Running stitch

■ Satin stitch

The Potting Shed Journal Cover Placement and Embroidery Pattern

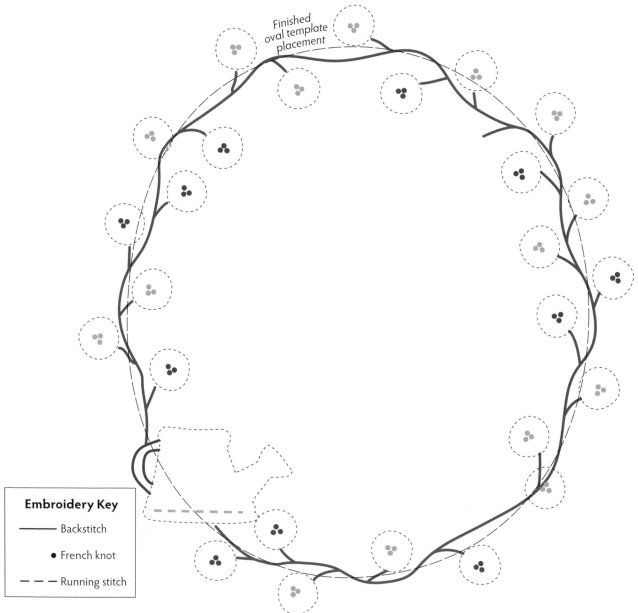

Finished
oval template
placement

Embroidery Key

——— Backstitch

● French knot

- - - Running stitch

Flower Placement and Vine Embroidery Pattern

Pencil Case

FINISHED SIZE
Approximately 8" × 5"

Materials

6 rectangles, 15" × 21" *each,* of coordinating prints or
checks for hexagons and zipper pull

12" × 12" square of cream fabric for pencil-case lining

5" × 6" rectangle of cream solid for oval embroidery
background*

4" × 5" scrap of red wool for oval embroidery frame

12" × 12" piece of lightweight fusible batting

Country red 6-strand embroidery floss (Cosmo #2241)

6" zipper and 3 tan buttons, ⅜" diameter, for zipper pull

5" × 6" rectangle of lightweight fusible embroidery
stabilizer, optional

Copy paper for pencil-case pattern

85 precut ¾" paper hexagons *OR* semi-water-soluble
appliqué paper hexagons**

Brown fine-tip fabric marker

Cardstock or template plastic

Water-soluble fabric-glue pen, optional

Water-soluble basting glue, optional

*If making both the pencil case and journal cover on page
80, cut both ovals from 1 fat eighth (9" × 21") of cream solid.*

**A ¾" hexagon template is provided on page 91 if you prefer
to cut your own hexagon papers using lightweight cardstock
or appliqué paper.*

Making the Outer Pencil Case

1 Using a pencil, trace the complete pencil-case
pattern on page 92 onto copy paper. You may need
to tape two pieces together to make a piece large
enough to trace the entire pattern.

2 Referring to "English-Paper-Pieced Hexagons" on
page 10 and using the fabric hexagon pattern on
page 91, cut 85 hexagons *total* from six coordinating
prints or checks. Glue or thread baste the fabric
hexagons to the paper hexagons.

3 Lay the hexagons flush in horizontal rows over the
paper pattern. Make sure all edges of the pattern are
covered (an area approximately 10" × 11") and the prints
are in a pleasing arrangement. Pin each hexagon to the
pencil-case pattern to maintain the placement.

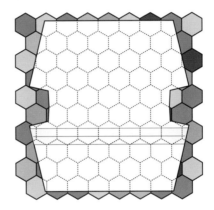

NO-PIN OPTION

*If you're not a fan of pins—they can be pokey en
masse—try double-sided sticky tape for keeping
hexagons in order for stitching. I put it in rows on the
paper pattern, then gently place the fabric-covered
hexies onto the tape. This way you don't lose the
placement, and the work is portable because the
tape keeps the hexies from moving!*

6 Using the pencil-case pattern, carefully cut out the patchwork for the outer pencil case. Also cut one piece from cream lining and one from batting. Transfer the zipper stop-and-start points from the pattern onto each piece with a fabric marker.

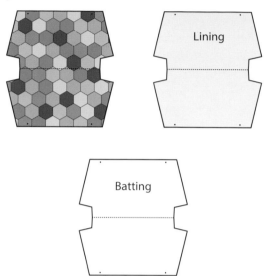

Cut 1 of each.

4 Join the hexagons, starting with the first two hexagons in the top row and working row by row. Place the two hexagons right sides together, along one flat edge. Take tiny whipstitches, carefully working the point of the needle through the folded edges while avoiding the paper.

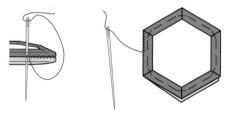

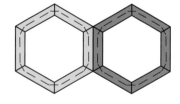

5 Once all the hexagons are joined, carefully remove all the papers.

7 Following the manufacturer's instructions, fuse the batting to the wrong side of the hexagon outer pencil case.

Embroidering the Oval

1 Using the placement and embroidery pattern on page 91, trace the oval shape onto the wrong side of the cream fabric. Do *not* cut out the oval.

2 Trace the embroidery design (page 91) onto the right side of the cream oval using a brown marker and light source and keeping the design ¼" from the oval outer edges. If using optional fusible embroidery stabilizer, fuse it to the wrong side of the fabric once the tracing is complete.

3 Referring to the embroidery key on page 91, work all the embroidery in red floss, noting the stitches used. Use one strand of floss for the beehive lines and chicken; use two strands for all other design elements. Once the embroidery is complete, press the work.

LYNETTE'S BEST-LOVED STITCHERIES

Preparing the Oval

1 Cut out the embroidered oval on the marked line. With the wrong side up, fold a ¼" seam allowance to the wrong side, basting in place as you go. Press gently.

2 Trace the oval pattern onto a piece of copy paper and cut it out. Using the pattern, cut an oval from the red wool. Do not turn under the seam allowance. Center the embroidered oval on the wool oval and pin or glue baste it in place.

3 Center the wool-backed oval on the outer pencil case, approximately 1" from the top edge. Appliqué the embroidered oval to the case through all layers. Leave the wool edges unstitched.

Appliqué placement

Making the Pencil Case

Use ¼" seam allowances. The zipper on the sample was inserted by hand, but the following instructions are for machine stitching to endure heavier use.

1 Place the outer pencil case right side up on a work surface. With the zipper open and the zipper pull on the right end, place the zipper face down with the zipper tape aligned with the raw edge and the zipper stop positioned at the marked starting point, as shown. If the distance between the zipper stops is beyond the zipper stop point on the pattern, you will need to shorten the zipper. See "Shortening a Nylon Zipper" above right. Stitch the zipper to the edge of the case, close to the zipper teeth. At the stop and start points, fold the zipper

tape ends away from the bag at an angle and catch in the stitching line.

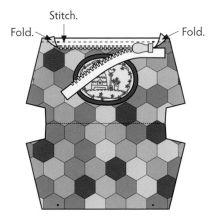

SHORTENING A NYLON ZIPPER

Note: This method should be used only for nylon zippers. Decide how long you need the zipper to be and mark the end point on the zipper tape. Set the sewing machine to a bar tack or zigzag stitch with a length of 0 and a width sufficient to clear the teeth. Center the zipper under the presser foot and slowly stitch back and forth to create a bar tack. Remove the zipper from the machine and cut off the end of the zipper approximately ½" from the bar tack.

2 Fold the case wrong sides together and pin the opposite side of the zipper to the remaining top edge. The right side of the zipper will be against the fabric. Make sure you align the zipper stop where indicated on the pattern; stitch.

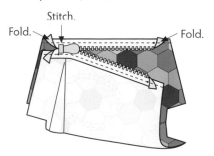

4 With the wrong side out, press one bottom corner of the case flat as shown. Stitch across the opening, backstitching on both sides to secure. Repeat to stitch the remaining corner of the case and both corners of the lining. Press both pieces. Fold ¼" along the top edge of the lining to the wrong side and press.

5 Turn the pencil case right side out, open the zipper completely, and insert the lining into the case, right sides together. Align the side seams and pin the lining to the case around the top edge so that the zipper tape is between the lining and the outside case. Stop pinning about ½" from the end of the zipper where it's joined to the case. Topstitch as close to the opened zipper pull as you can, stitching around the top of the case and back to the zipper pull and being careful not to stitch through any zipper teeth.

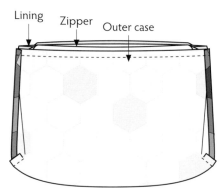

6 If desired, close the small openings on each side of the zipper with a hand tack stitch using two strands of floss to match the fabric.

Making the Yo-Yo Zipper Pull

1 Trace the yo-yo pattern on page 91 onto cardstock or template plastic. Cut it out.

2 Using the template and the brown marker, draw around the template on the wrong side of four different print scraps. Cut out the circles on the marked lines.

3 Thread a sewing needle with regular cotton sewing thread and knot one end.

3 With the zipper installed (and still open) and the case wrong sides together, pin and stitch both side seams. Fold and stitch the sides of the lining in the same manner. Press the seam allowances open.

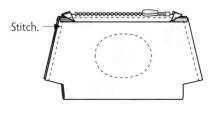

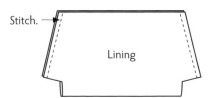

4 With the wrong side of the circle facing you, turn under and stitch down the ⅛" seam allowance, gathering it gently to shape the yo-yo. Keep the running stitches fairly small to leave a nice-sized opening in the center of the yo-yo. Once you're happy with the yo-yo shape, pull the thread firmly and tie off the thread on the back. Repeat to make four yo-yos.

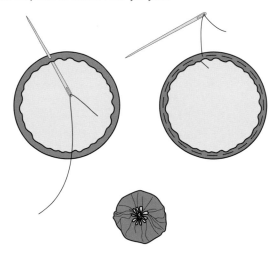

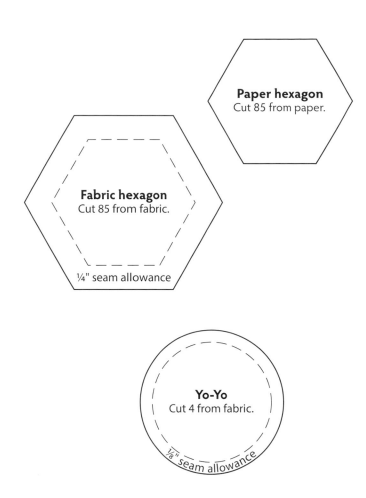

Paper hexagon
Cut 85 from paper.

Fabric hexagon
Cut 85 from fabric.

¼" seam allowance

Yo-Yo
Cut 4 from fabric.

⅛" seam allowance

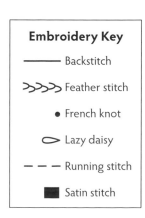

5 Alternate the four finished yo-yos with three tan buttons (I used vintage ones from my button jar). Thread them together through the centers using two strands of red floss, and attach the unit to the zipper pull as decoration.

Oval template placement.

Embroidery Key

——— Backstitch

>>>> Feather stitch

• French knot

◠ Lazy daisy

– – – Running stitch

▬ Satin stitch

The Potting Shed Pencil Case

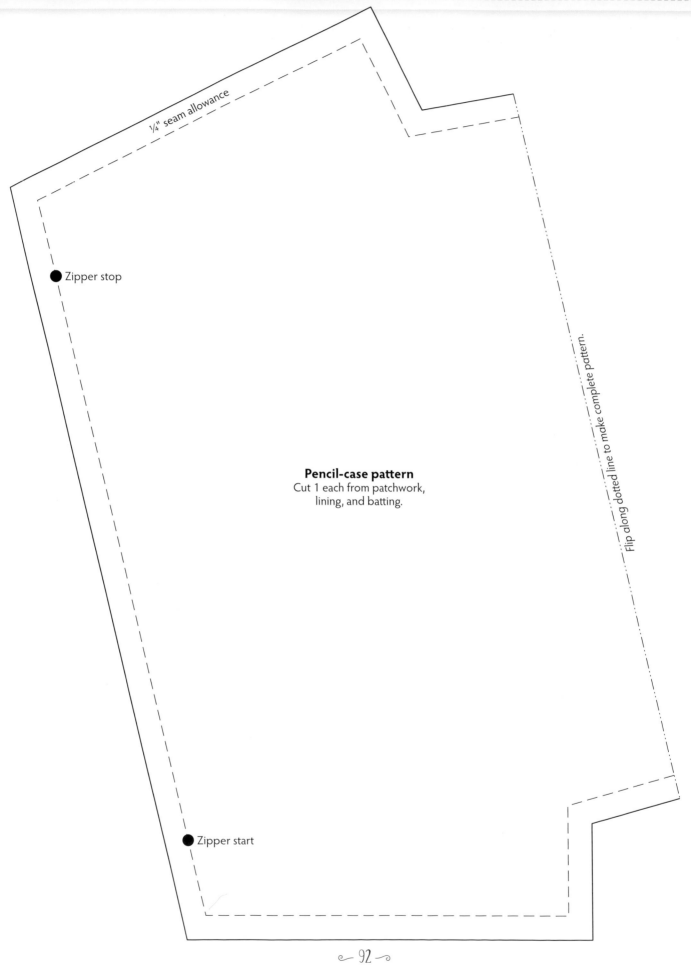

¼" seam allowance

● Zipper stop

Pencil-case pattern
Cut 1 each from patchwork,
lining, and batting.

Flip along dotted line to make complete pattern.

● Zipper start

Home Sweet Home Redwork

Designed with a primitive house button as the focal point, this framed redwork sampler displays beautifully with the other two redwork pieces in this book—the Bee an Angel and All Birds Welcome pillows on page 30. There's nothing quite as calming and addictive as redwork.

FINISHED SIZE
3" × 6½" (unframed)

Materials

8" × 8" square of cream solid for embroidery background

Country red 6-strand embroidery floss (Cosmo #2241)

1" × 2" house button (YB304 Simply Stitches Button Pack from Lynette Anderson Designs)

6⅛" × 9¾" wooden frame with 2⅞" × 6⅜" interior opening*

Loose tea leaves, optional

8" × 8" square of fusible embroidery stabilizer, optional

Brown fine-tip fabric marker

The wooden frame shown was custom-made at a frame shop to fit the embroidery.

Embroidering the Square

1 To dye the cream fabric for the speckled effect shown, refer to page 30.

2 Trace the embroidery pattern on page 95 onto the right side of the cream square, using a brown marker and a light source. If using optional fusible embroidery stabilizer, fuse it to the wrong side of the fabric once the tracing is complete.

3 Referring to the embroidery key on page 95, work all the embroidery in one strand of red floss, noting the stitches used. If you prefer, choose blue or green floss to suit your color scheme.

4 Press the completed embroidery and trim the square to 3" × 6½", centering the embroidery.

5 Stitch the button in the center of the embroidery referring to the pattern for placement. Frame the redwork as shown or use as the center embroidery on a larger project.

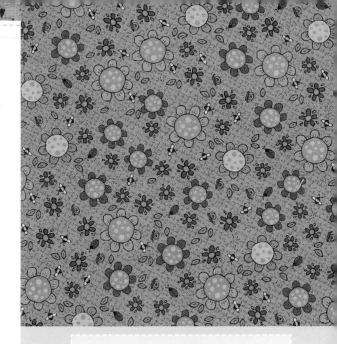

Home Sweet Home Embroidery Pattern

Text inside pattern:
Home is where the heart is

Button placement

a b c d e f g h i j k l m
n o p q r s t u v w x y z

Home Sweet Home

Embroidery Key

——— Backstitch

✗ Cross-stitch

• French knot

◡ Lazy daisy

– – – Running stitch

▬ Satin stitch

RESOURCES

If you can't find the tools and materials you need at your local quilt shop or retailer, you can order Apliquick tools, a nonslip design mat, hand-painted buttons, plastic domes, zippers, wooden frames, Cosmo and Valdani embroidery floss, appliqué paper, Lynette's fabrics, and more at:

Little Quilt Store
PO Box 9314
Pacific Paradise
QLD 4564
Australia

+ 61 7 5450 7497
sales@littlequiltstore.com.au
LittleQuiltStore.com.au

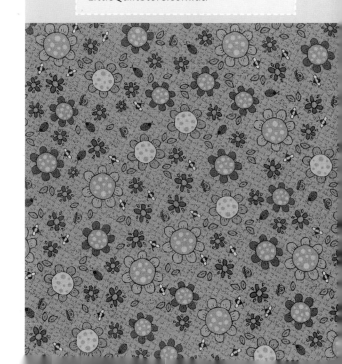

About the Author

Lynette Anderson's love affair with textiles began at a young age. She grew up in a small village in Dorset, England, where her grandmothers taught her to embroider and knit. Patchwork caught her attention in 1981 after the birth of her first son. She moved with her family to Australia in 1990, which prompted the release of her first patterns in 1995. During the ensuing years Lynette has produced hundreds of patterns.

Her distinctive and appealing design style, which combines simple stitchery with appliqué and piecing, attracts stitchers worldwide. Inspired by nature, childhood events, and her beloved pets, she enjoys designing quilts, pillows, bags, and sewing accessories.

Lynette's hand-painted wooden buttons and the fabric collections she has designed for Lecien Fabrics are the perfect complements to her creative style. She splits her time between designing at her home studio and working in the warehouse dispatching pattern orders. One of her greatest passions is teaching, and Lynette enjoys traveling the world to share her designs with her students.

For more information, visit:

LittleQuiltStore.com.au
LynetteAndersonDesigns.typepad.com
Facebook.com/LynetteAndersonDesigns
Instagram: @lynetteandersondesigns